Pedagogical Supervision

Relational Supervision

Pedagogical Supervision

A Competency Standards Framework

Yamina Bouchamma,
Marc Giguère, and Daniel April

ROWMAN & LITTLEFIELD
Lanham • Boulder • New York • London

Published by Rowman & Littlefield
An imprint of The Rowman & Littlefield Publishing Group, Inc.
4501 Forbes Boulevard, Suite 200, Lanham, Maryland 20706
www.rowman.com

6 Tinworth Street, London SE11 5AL, United Kingdom

Copyright © 2019 by Yamina Bouchamma, Marc Giguère, and Daniel April

All rights reserved. No part of this book may be reproduced in any form or by any electronic or mechanical means, including information storage and retrieval systems, without written permission from the publisher, except by a reviewer who may quote passages in a review.

British Library Cataloguing in Publication Information Available

Library of Congress Cataloging-in-Publication Data Is Available

ISBN 978-1-4758-5067-3 (cloth: alk. paper)
ISBN 978-1-4758-5068-0 (pbk: alk. paper)
ISBN 978-1-4758-5069-7 (electronic)

Leadership is the capacity to translate vision into reality.
—Warren Bennis

Contents

List of Figures and Tables	ix
Preface	xi
Introduction	xiii

PART I: SUPERVISION CONTEXT OF THE PEDAGOGICAL SUPERVISOR — 1

1 Competence — 3

2 Pedagogical Supervision: Developing Teacher Competence — 7
   2.1—The Systemic Approach in Pedagogical Supervision — 8
   2.2—Pedagogical Supervision: A Definition — 8

3 The Skills of the Pedagogical Supervisor — 11
   3.1—Two Types of Skills — 11
   3.2—Six Transversal Skills — 12

PART II: COMPETENCY STANDARDS FRAMEWORK — 19

4 The Knowledge for Effective Supervision — 21
   4.1—Pedagogical Knowledge — 21
   4.2—Knowledge in Human Relations — 27

5 The *Know How to Do* Every Supervisor Should Possess — 33
   5.1—Pedagogical *Know How to Do* — 33
   5.2—*Know How to Do* in Human Relations — 45

6 The *Know How to Be* Every Supervisor Should Possess — 59
   6.1—Pedagogical *Know How to Be* — 59
   6.2—*Know How to Be* in Human Relations — 60

7	The *Know How to Become* Every Supervisor Should Possess	71
	7.1—Pedagogical *Know How to Become*	72
	7.2—*Know How to Become* in Human Relations	73
Conclusion		75
References		77
About the Authors		89

List of Figures and Tables

Figure 1.1.	The Four Dimensions of Competence	5
Figure 1.2.	The Definition of Competence	5
Figure 2.1.	From Pedagogical Supervision to Student Achievement	7
Figure 2.2.	Overview of Pedagogical Supervision	10
Figure 3.1.	Essential Skills of a Pedagogical Supervisor	14
Table 3.1.	Competencies of the Effective Supervisor	15
Table 4.1.	Types of Supervision Models	25
Figure 4.1.	Management Styles from Most to Least Controlling	30
Table 4.2.	Synthesis of the Main Knowledge for Effective Supervision	31
Table 5.1.	Conceptualization and Categorization of School Climate	49
Table 5.2.	Synthesis of the Main *Know How to Do* of the Effective Supervisor	57
Figure 6.1.	Equality versus Equity	63
Figure 6.2.	The Barrel Metaphor	66
Table 6.1.	A Comparison of Sympathy and Empathy	66
Table 6.2.	Synthesis of the Main *Know How to Be* of an Effective Supervisor	69
Table 7.1.	Synthesis of the Main *Know How to Become* of the Effective Supervisor	74

Preface

In 2017, I published with Marc Giguère and Daniel April a first edition of this book, in French. Marc has a very good knowledge of the school environment. He worked as a teacher, a school principal (primary and secondary), and a lecturer in the training of school administrators (Université Laval). During his time as a principal, he experimented with and implemented various models of individual and collective pedagogical supervision.

Daniel, a PhD student in the field of pedagogical supervision, has held the position of academic director for the French immersion program at Université Sainte-Anne in Nova Scotia. He is also a research and communications consultant for the Global Education Monitoring Report published by UNESCO.

As a professor-teacher at both the University of Moncton and the University Laval, I gained significant experience supervising teachers, which motivated me to begin this book.

Due to a grant from the Quebec Ministry of Education (Canada), we were able to set up professional learning communities (PLCs) with school principals on two Quebec school boards. The objective of these PLCs was to support these principals in the establishment and development of individual and collective educational supervision practices in their schools.

Our different experiences in teaching, management, and research on pedagogical supervision have been very useful in this project. Together, we collaborated to collect, analyze, and conceptualize the principals' practices in supervision. The results of this research-action-training project have allowed several other principals to put in place a more structured model of teacher supervision.

This book is now the key text used in my Pedagogical Management and Supervision course. This course is intended for use by principals and master's degree and doctoral students.

Yamina Bouchamma

Introduction

Over the last few decades, the *accountability movement* has made its way into the school setting, with many countries introducing results-driven reforms in education. The ultimate goal of this management system is to improve student achievement by measuring the efficacy of actions and their coherence. Measurable goals thus serve to "pilot" the education system, refocus school-teams on their respective priorities, and better regulate school processes and operations.

In the early twenty-first century, a renewal of supervisory practices began. Indeed, results-based management policies cannot be successfully implemented in schools without first establishing a systematic system of pedagogical supervision. In many education systems, the school principal is the person who is legally responsible for supervision, while in others, this duty may fall on another individual (pedagogical advisor, department head, school inspector, etc.). In any case, the term *supervisor* is used to designate the person *whose leadership pursues and facilitates professional learning*.

The role of pedagogical leader is necessarily exercised through supervision, which ultimately leads to the improvement of education services for students and ensures a positive impact on the latter's achievement, both quantitatively and qualitatively. This type of supervision operates within an administrative process that includes planning, organization, execution and coordination, supervision, assessment, and accountability.

As an integral part of quality teaching, pedagogical supervision enables the supervisor to effectively support their school-team as they grow professionally and reflect on their practice.

Historically, pedagogical supervision has evolved through different models, with varying levels of control over the person being supervised. Some have viewed supervision as a process involving authority, control, even intimidation (Sullivan & Glanz, 2000). In recent years, however, the paradigm has shifted toward a more open, collegial approach (Witherspoon Arnold, 2016; Zepeda, 2013). In chapter 2, a definition of *pedagogical supervision* is proposed focusing on professional development and not limited only to pedagogical supervision.

Along with other authors, we examine supervision through its formative dimension in the perspective of professional growth. Our view of supervision centers on the needs of the teachers—rather than on those of the organization—where supervision is a necessary function that supports the professional development of teachers and the enrichment of teaching practices.

The supervisor uses pedagogical supervision to guide, accompany, and coach teachers in how to collect and analyze relevant data to adjust and improve teaching practices. This ongoing, nonjudgmental, and collaborative process involves professionals in the improvement of their practices. Supervision thus constitutes a key element to enhance teaching quality and student learning by focusing on the teachers' level of involvement in the process.

However, pedagogical supervision is complex and multidimensional, with a series of challenges along the way on more than one level (organizational, practical, socioaffective, and conceptual). The perceptions and beliefs of education stakeholders are also spiked with ambiguities. Supervisors tend to believe that supervision is universal, with a commonly shared definition; such is not the case for the persons being supervised who often mistrust any changes in how they are assessed.

Bearing this in mind, what kind of expertise should supervisors develop to be effective in situations of individual and collective pedagogical supervision? In this competency standards framework, we propose that supervisors address this question by examining the professional competence of supervisors through various forms of knowledge.

We thus examine supervision in terms of competence in four types of knowledge in pedagogical supervision, namely, knowledge (*know-what*), *know how to do*, *know how to be*, and *know how to become*. We then broaden our investigation toward professional competence associated with pedagogical supervision.

This work contributes by enriching existing knowledge on the skills required to exercise effective pedagogical supervision but more importantly by better positioning the actions of school leaders in this area. Indeed, this skills reference manual was conceived and designed with and for education practitioners, thereby emphasizing originality and worth. This competency standards framework is also timely, as reference frameworks and established policies in pedagogical supervision are lacking. Supervisors who use this book will thus be better equipped to improve their support practices and adjust their professional development accordingly.

Initially, this work was presented in French following a needs analysis emanating from a research-action-training project (2014–2017) conducted in two Québec school districts. Although all of the participating school leaders recognized the importance of supervision and considered it to be an important and integral part of their duties as school principal, 65% of them ($n = 37$) admitted having never received initial or professional development training in pedagogical supervision. In this context, they were interested in learning more on the subject to enhance their level of expertise and be better prepared to provide effective supervision. Finally, this work represents a global approach that is not exclusive to only one education system.

PRELIMINARY REMARKS

- We intentionally use certain key works to clearly and precisely document the presented theme to enable supervisors to acquire or update these necessary skills in pedagogical supervision.
- The school principal is usually responsible for pedagogical supervision; in some areas, however, another person may be in charge (vice principal, department head, district inspector, etc.).
- While the term *school district* is employed in this reference manual to designate the authority responsible for schools in a given territory, some countries/provinces use other designations, such as education council, school board, school division, Department of Education, or local education officials. In some jurisdictions, school districts may be divided based on linguistic or religious criteria. In Canada and the United States, school districts are generally administered directly by popular-vote-elected members.

Part I

SUPERVISION CONTEXT OF THE PEDAGOGICAL SUPERVISOR

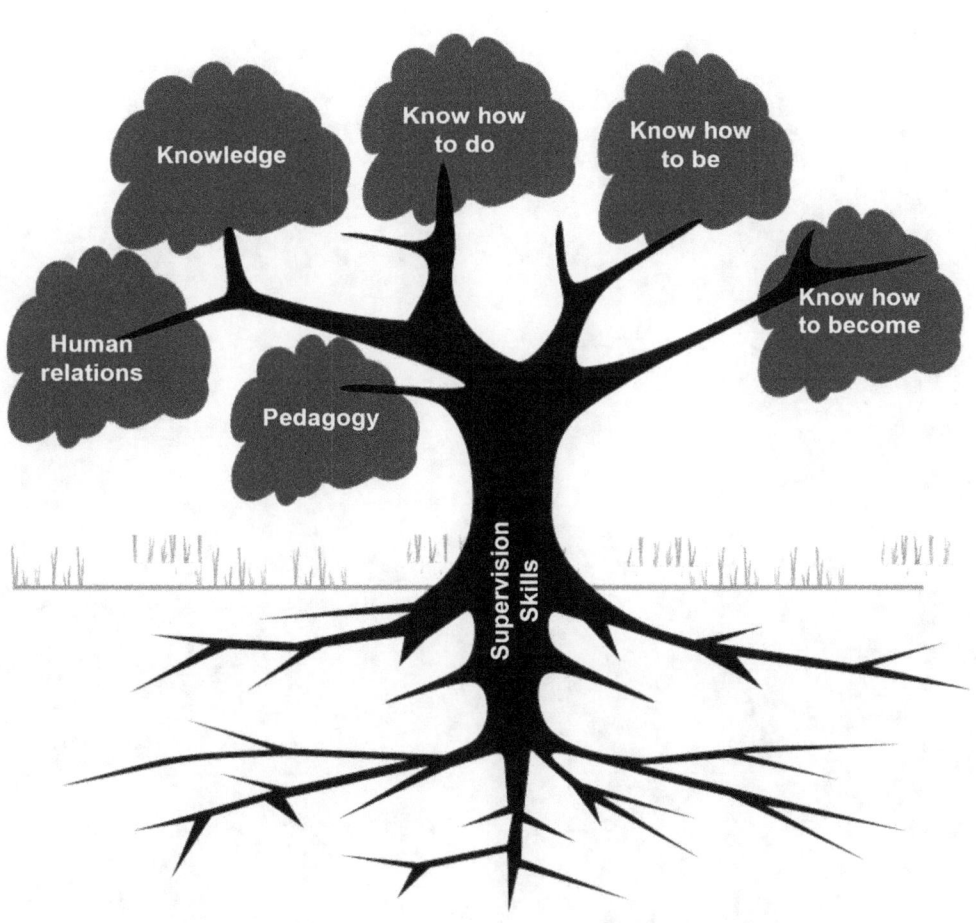

Chapter One

Competence

Competence can be defined as the skill or ability to act effectively in a job or situation and to exercise responsibility. In other words, it is the ability to mobilize an integrated cluster of knowledge, skills, and attitudes to perform or achieve a given task or function at a predetermined level of performance, according to desired standards and outcomes (Legendre, 2005).

Further to these capabilities or abilities to accomplish a specific function is the notion of complexity, of *knowing how to act* or react. This empirical knowledge is employed in actual work-related contexts and adapts to each given situation. This knowledge is characterized by a series of combined actions deployed toward the attainment of a goal and by lifelong professional development and reflection.

Le Boterf (2011) added the notions of *wanting to act* and *knowing how to act*. Wanting to act is actualized through the meaning given to the construction of skills, a realistic and positive self-image, recognition and trust, and the enhancement of competence. Knowing how to act takes place through an organization of work that enables and facilitates the deployment of skills and the necessary means to legitimize the development of capabilities, as well as through a network of relational and documentary resources.

Knowledge can be memorized. Indeed, theoretical, contextual, and procedural knowledge serve to understand, describe, explain an object or a situation, and introduce action. This knowledge is formalized and can be transmitted to each learner (Le Boterf, 2002).

Similar to Drucker (1966), Toffler (1990), and Quinn (1992), pioneers in the study of knowledge in work contexts, Duffy (2016) concurred that knowledge constitutes "the" resource, "the" source of power, and "the" key to change.

Abilities arise from *know-how*, from integrating and using knowledge in the practice, including tricks of the trade, tactics, and conscious activities, whether intentional or deliberate. They are technical skills related to experience in the exercise of professional activity (Legendre, 2005).

Attitudes define the nature or the state of mind of the individual: *knowing how to be*. According to Lebrun, Smidts, and Bricoult (2011), *knowing how to be* refers to how a professional views themselves within the realm of values, attitudes, and behaviors in terms of context, their position within this context, their personal reaction to problems, and lastly, regarding others. *Knowing how to be* makes it possible to use our personal resources (aptitudes, qualities, emotions, or physiological attributes) in a given situation (Le Boterf, 2002).

Knowledge, *knowing how to do*, and *knowing how to be* make up a series of interdependent elements integrated within the notion of competence. In fact, this is among the most widely accepted definitions (Courpasson & Livian, 1991; Durand, 2000, in Loufrani-Fedida, & Saint-Germes, 2013). Despite much criticism, the main interest in this conception of competence remains its nature, which is didactic, practical, and easy to understand and to remember (Loufrani-Fedida & Saint-Germes, 2013).

That said, with the ever-evolving context and the emergence of multiple new forms of knowledge, it is our view that the aforementioned knowledge/*know how to do*/*know how to be* no longer suffice to fully define *competence*.

Along with Loufrani-Fedida and Saint-Germes (2013) and Dupuich-Rabasse (2006), we deem it of importance to complete these three types of knowledge with a fourth type, namely, *knowing how to become* within a temporal, evolving, and dynamic perspective. Although this form of knowledge has rarely been explored in reference manuals, Lebrun, Smidts, and Bricoult (2011) viewed this component as the manner in which we seek to influence the course of things and give meaning to our future. *Knowing how to become* involves a commitment to our professional development and that of others. Hallier (2009) put forth that this new context has led professionals to engage individually and collectively within a continuous and sustainable process of self-development and mobility. *Knowing how to become* ensures competent action in our practice and that of each staff member and team within the organization, and enhances the development of our capabilities and those of each staff member.

This conception of competence does vary, however, in the literature. For example, Quinn, Anderson, and Finkelstein (1996, in Duffy, 2016) identified the same two aforementioned levels of competence, referred to as "professional intellect":

- *know-what* or cognitive knowledge obtained through training and certification;
- *know-how*, which enables the transfer from theory to practice.

However, these authors also identified two new dimensions that are less common in recent literature:

- *know-why*, an understanding of systems that develops a profound knowledge of the causes and enables one to solve important and complex problems;
- *care-why*, which enables a person to be proactive rather than reactive.

Figure 1.1 presents the four interdependent dimensions of competence.

Figure 1.2 schematically illustrates the concept of competence by uniting and articulating these four dimensions, namely, knowledge, *know how to do*, *know how to be*, and *know how to become*.

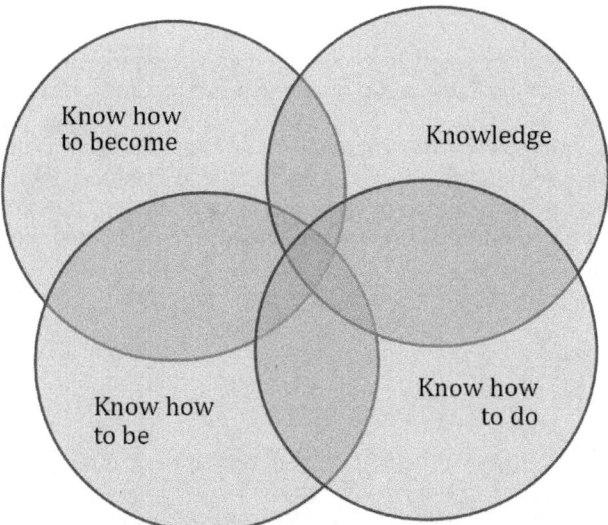

Figure 1.1. The Four Dimensions of Competence
Original figure created by the authors

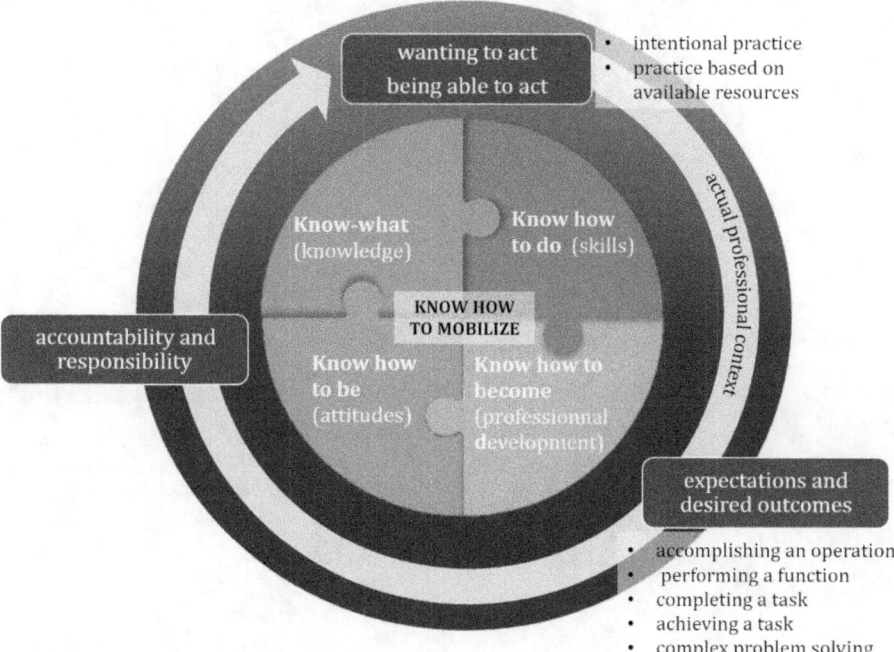

Figure 1.2. The Definition of Competence
Original figure created by the authors

We use the following definition in this work:

> Competence is a complex *know-how-to-act* in a concrete professional context. It pertains to the ability to mobilize a group of interdependent forms of knowledge, namely, *know-what* (knowledge), *know how to do* (skills), *know how to be* (attitudes), and *know how to become* (professional development) to ensure competent actions. It emerges from an intention (wanting to act) and from available resources (being able to act). *Competent action* refers to accomplishing a task or operation, performing a duty, or achieving a goal based on established expectations and anticipated outcomes.

Chapter Two

Pedagogical Supervision
Developing Teacher Competence

With the emergence of the effective school movement, schools are now considered to have the power to counterbalance the effect of other achievement indicators (socioeconomic and cultural). The school-effect thus unfolds on the front line through the teachers, who must receive the appropriate guidance and pedagogical supervision to be able to successfully do their job.

Figure 2.1 indicates the direct effect (solid lines) and indirect effect (dotted lines) of pedagogical supervision on student achievement.

In light of this, which skills should a supervisor have to be more pedagogically effective? This chapter identifies this pedagogical expertise based on research in the field of pedagogical supervision and on the results of a research-action-training initiative conducted with effective school principals and vice principals.

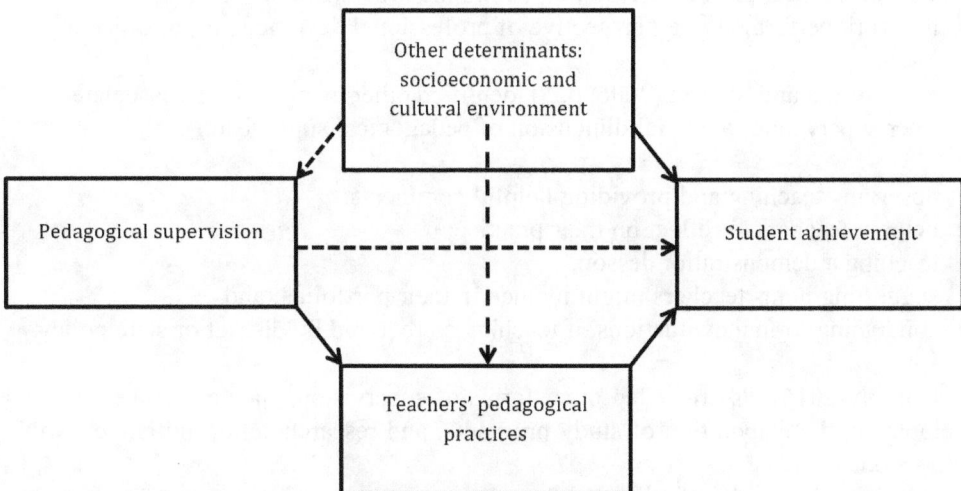

Figure 2.1. From Pedagogical Supervision to Student Achievement
Original figure created by the authors

2.1—THE SYSTEMIC APPROACH IN PEDAGOGICAL SUPERVISION

Although pedagogical supervision takes place inside the school, the systemic approach is in fact a more global technique in which all of the education stakeholders work toward a common goal, which is student achievement.

In many education systems, school district authorities or superintendents provide support for their principals in a perspective of assistance and professional development.

The supervisor supports their teachers and serves as facilitator to ensure their professional development and the improvement of education services for the students. In the classroom, the teacher not only teaches their subject and conducts summative and formative student evaluations but also sees to the students' overall development by proposing additional activities when necessary to attain the learning objectives. Pedagogical supervision thus takes place on different levels, with each level feeding the next level in a systemic manner.

2.2—PEDAGOGICAL SUPERVISION: A DEFINITION

Pedagogical supervision is an approach characterized by discussions with and support for a person or group of persons. A critical analysis is performed during ongoing actions or processes on one of the following aspects:

- the education services provided by the staff;
- the organization's priorities;
- the actions inherent to an operation, group of operations, or mandate;
- the pedagogical projects developed within the organization;
- the work performed in a perspective of professional development; or others.

Sergiovanni and Starratt (2006, p. 5) identified other manifestations associated with teacher supervision (a crucial dimension of pedagogical supervision):

- observing teaching and providing helpful comments;
- helping teachers to reflect on their practice;
- teaching a demonstration lesson;
- suggesting items teachers might include in their portfolios; and
- conducting formal evaluations of teaching as required by district or state policy.

Gordon (2016) also revealed other forms of supervision, such as professional development, the elaboration of study programs, and research-action initiatives within the school.

Based on the results of collected data and facts, pedagogical supervision is undertaken either formally or informally to enhance ongoing processes and actions and to introduce the necessary changes to attain the desired outcomes. The point of pedagogical supervision is thus to improve the educational services for the students and the latter's qualitative and quantitative achievement.

This definition emanates from the administrative process commonly known in school management.

Principles of Pedagogical Supervision

Burns, Yendol-Hoppey, and Jacobs (2015) identified the fundamental principles of pedagogical supervision.

1. Pedagogical supervision requires the recognition, respect, and development of a complex set of knowledge and skills. It also commands social justice.
2. Unification is key in pedagogical supervision and yet is complicated because of the numerous organizational units involved (schools, departments, curricula, training programs, etc.), the many needs and objectives of the various organizations, and the capacity of the members to commit.
3. Supervision must be differentiated to address the development needs of the teachers and other stakeholders. This requires addressing the developmental differences and being on top of effective learning and professional development theories. Differentiated supervision also requires an understanding of the cognitive, emotional, and physical dimensions of the persons being supervised.
4. Supervision must provide the members of the community with various individual and collective growth opportunities.

Nolan and Hoover (2004) reiterated the importance of a climate of community, collaboration, and continuous growth, and emphasized the need to consider both the characteristics of the supervised teachers and their career paths.

Finally, in their examination of five works published between 2000 and 2005, Burke and Krey (2005) identified several key concepts associated with the various definitions of pedagogical supervision: collegiality and collaboration among the teachers, the improvement of teaching quality and student achievement, a focus on the professional growth and development of teachers, and the reinforcement of teacher participation and commitment in the attainment of the school's objectives and those of their district.

The Individual and Collective Approach

Individual supervision consists of guiding and supporting a teacher in their teaching practices and professional development and of evaluating only those teachers who are nonpermanent, who experience difficulty, or who are difficult. Collective supervision is used to facilitate small or large groups in their discussion and sharing of professional practices and knowledge (among others), to readjust the members' focus and actions, and to support the professional development of teachers. This form of supervision may be proposed in the context of a pedagogical project, an action plan, or an operation or group of operations toward such things as the implementation of a new program or model or the experimentation of new didactic material.

10   Chapter Two

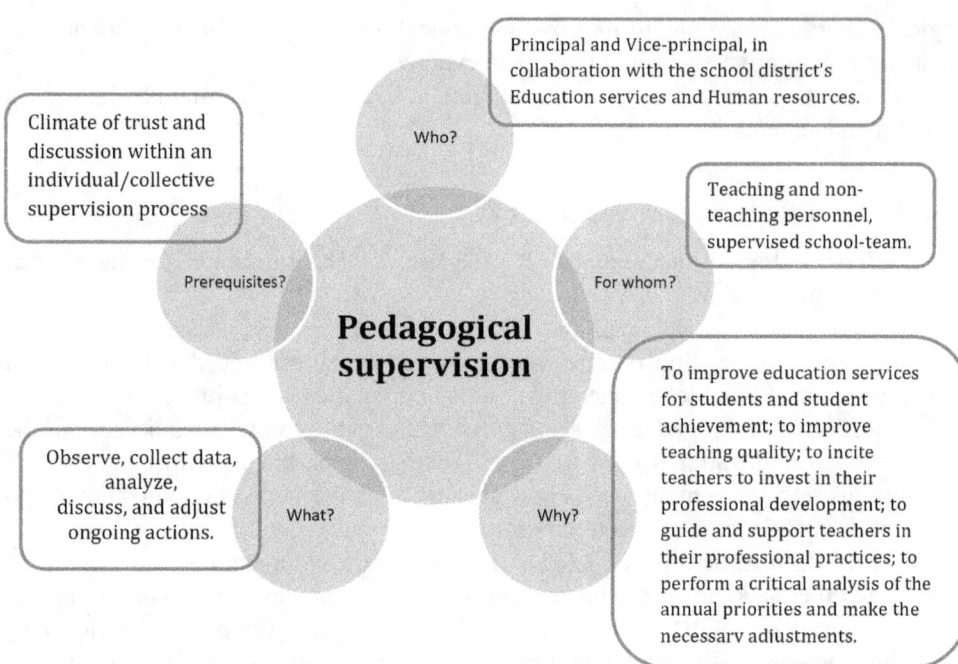

Figure 2.2. Overview of Pedagogical Supervision
Original figure created by the authors

Figure 2.2 summarizes the concept of pedagogical supervision based on five dimensions: prerequisites, who, what, for whom, and why. The supervisor (who) must first establish a climate of trust and discussion (prerequisites). The supervisor then undertakes supervision actions (what) with the supervised person (for whom) with the ultimate goal of improving student outcomes (why).

Chapter Three

The Skills of the Pedagogical Supervisor

In this chapter, we examine two types of competencies, namely, pedagogical skills and human relations skills, as well as six transversal or core skills in pedagogical supervision: leadership, method, cooperation, communication, ethics, and emotional intelligence.

3.1—TWO TYPES OF SKILLS

Glanz and Zepeda (2015) identified interpersonal, pedagogical, and technical skills in pedagogical supervision. The *interpersonal skills* of the supervisor favor relationships with, between, and among the teachers. These skills become more complex, however, when supervisors work to establish a relationship of trust and collaboration between several individuals or groups of individuals. The *pedagogical skills* of the supervisor make it possible to improve the practices and educational services toward the improvement of student outcomes. Lastly, the supervisor's *technical skills* include such abilities as collecting and analyzing data, observing, planning, and evaluating.

In light of this study, our previous work on the subject of teacher supervision (Bouchamma, Giguère, & April, 2016), and the results emanating from our research-action-training project (2014–2017) conducted in a practice community with school principals, we retained two types of skills required for effective teacher supervision, namely, pedagogical skills and human relations skills. The technical skills have been included in the *know how to do* capabilities (as well as in the core skills) along with the other forms of competence (knowledge, *know how to be*, and *know how to become*).

3.1.1—Pedagogical Skills

The pedagogical skills every supervisor should have are knowledge, *know how to do*, *know how to be*, and *know how to become*. Using these skills makes it possible to pursue three key objectives: encourage the professional and pedagogical development of the school-team, perfect educational actions, and improve student achievement.

3.1.2—Human Relations Skills

Teachers' perceptions of supervision vary depending on their experiences. In fact, when we think about supervision we may have experienced, what we remember most is probably what affected us personally. We most likely remember an experience, an attitude, or a discussion that generated a positive or negative attitude on our part. In essence, one could say that the heart of pedagogical supervision lies in its relational aspect.

Human relations skills involve three abilities related to emotional intelligence: self-esteem, self-control, and social conscience. These skills define the aptitude we have to use our awareness regarding our emotions and that of others to effectively manage our interactions. This ability enhances clarity in what is being communicated (Bradberry & Greaves, 2009).

3.2—SIX TRANSVERSAL SKILLS

Pedagogical supervision competence houses six transversal skills: leadership, method, cooperation, communication, ethics, and emotional intelligence.

3.2.1—Leadership

Leadership refers to the function or role of a person who heads a group or organization. It also encompasses all of the actions deployed by this person to influence the actions and behaviors of others (Legendre, 2005). In other words, it the ability to have a clear vision of the changes to be undertaken coupled with the ability to influence and lead others toward this vision.

In the realm of school administration, *leadership* refers to all of the behaviors and practices used by school leaders to influence their school-team and unite them around a common project, educational objectives, general objectives, and a collective action plan. Effective school leaders thus demonstrate innovativeness, creativity, and adaptability.

3.2.2—Method

According to Legendre (2005), a method is a system using successful techniques that are organized according to rules and consciously deployed to reach a specific goal. It is the regulatory mode of operation to solve problems and get results.

The supervisor follows a rigorously structured approach that enables them to oversee the transfer of each type of knowledge (*know-what*, *know how to do*, *know how to be*, and *know how to become*) in every situation involving supervision. Here, the method requires data collection, the determination of priorities, elaboration and implementation, and the supervision and evaluation of an action plan.

3.2.3—Cooperation

Cooperation refers to a concerted mode of action involving one or more partners toward a common goal. Here, the focus is on helping, facilitating, or completing a partner's task (Legendre, 2005). The elements leading to collaboration are, in order: social interaction, peer consultation, professional cooperation, and mentoring (Riordan & Da Costa, 1996).

Cooperation is associated with collaboration. Indeed, the literature often uses these concepts interchangeably, as is evidenced by such concepts as cooperation, collaboration, and collegiality (McEwan, 1997), or the six stages leading from isolation to collegiality: autocracy, coordination, accommodation, independence, cooperation, and collaboration (Howden & Kopiec, 2002). Other authors have structured these concepts along a continuum going from isolation (independence) to collaboration (interdependence).

Cooperation occurs in the form of connections and behaviors through which a relationship is created between supervisor and the supervised person to enable harmonious exchange and the identification, together, of the appropriate means to move toward effective solutions.

3.2.4—Communication

The communication process takes place between a sender (encoding) and a receiver (decoding) through a verbal or nonverbal canal. *Communication* refers to the emission and reception of messages that carry meaning (Schermerhorn, Hunt, Osborn, & de Billy, 2014). It is thus designed to be interactive, where each behavior has the value of a message (Rousseau, 2005).

In the school setting, the supervisor establishes good communication by ensuring the construction of a common meaning and language and the sharing of their (oral and written) vision. The effective supervisor uses clear communication to mobilize the school-team around orientations and objectives. This communication also stimulates the sharing of individual and collective teaching practices and helps generate discussions that nurture the professional development of teachers.

3.2.5—Ethics

Whether in a context of individual or group supervision, the supervisor must be increasingly mindful when it comes to ethics. A good supervisor establishes a management culture founded on transparency, accountability, impartiality, ethics, and responsibility, among others, and is devoted to ensuring a harmonious work environment, pursuing the common good, and demonstrating daily behaviors and attitudes that adhere to high moral standards.

3.2.6—Emotional Intelligence

Another important dimension of human skills is emotional intelligence, or the aptitude enabling a person to work well with others.

In addition to the rational dimension, the supervisor must consider the emotional and affective dimension of the person or persons being supervised. Emotional intelligence is the capacity to understand our own self and effectively manage our own

14   *Chapter Three*

emotions and relationships with others. The main components of this form of intelligence have been extensively researched. For example, Schermerhorn, Hunt, Osborn, and de Billy (2015) described them as follows:

- Self-awareness: the ability to understand our emotions and the impact they have on ourselves and others;
- Social awareness: empathy for and understanding of the emotions of others and their impact on relationships;
- Self-management: self-regulation, self-control, thinking before doing, and controlling our emotions;
- Relationship management: establishing a good rapport with others, using emotions to strengthen and maintain good relationships.

Figure 3.1 illustrates the two types of skills of a pedagogical supervisor, namely, pedagogical skills and human relations skills. For a more global appreciation of these two essential components of effective pedagogical supervision, the six core skills have also been included.

Table 3.1 presents all of the knowledge, *know how to do*, *know how to be*, and *know how to become* examined in this work.

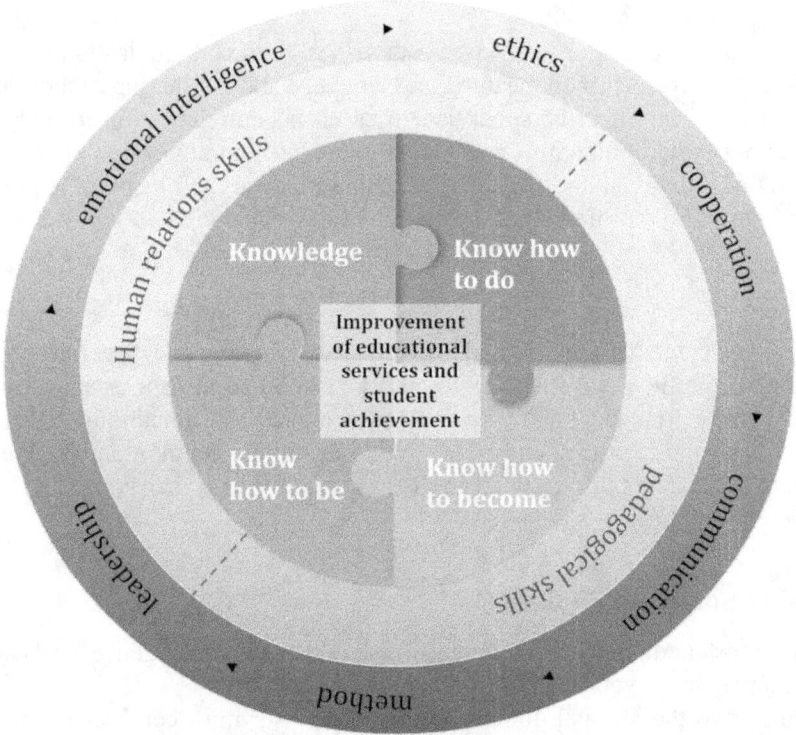

Figure 3.1. Essential Skills of a Pedagogical Supervisor
Original figure created by the authors

Table 3.1. Competencies of the Effective Supervisor

Knowledge	
Pedagogically	*In Human Relations*
4.1.1. Have a pedagogical vision and educational values.	4.2.1 Know the organizational culture and particularities of the work environment.
4.1.2 Know the national and local policies pertaining to teacher supervision.	4.2.2 Know the personal and professional profile of each supervised teacher.
4.1.3 Know my school's issues regarding student achievement.	4.2.3 Know my leadership and management styles.
4.1.4 Know the resources provided by education services to support my teacher supervision practice.	4.2.4 Know the services provided by human resources to support my teacher supervision practice.
4.1.5 Know the basic principles of pedagogical supervision.	4.2.5 Know facilitation techniques.

Know How to Do	
Pedagogically	*In Human Relations*
Leadership:	**Leadership:**
5.1.1 Use pedagogical leadership: Promote my vision of the school system, my educational orientations and values; encourage the professional development of my staff; support pedagogical projects and innovations.	5.2.1 Use relational leadership: Encourage communication, consultation, and discussion among the teachers.
	5.2.2 Use transformational leadership: Inspire, stimulate, optimize the potential of each teacher, and empower them toward self-reliance.
5.1.2 Use situational leadership: Focus on the students' needs and the school's education priorities.	5.2.3 Delegate support duties and responsibilities to the vice principal and to teachers and closely monitor.
5.1.3 Manage ethnocultural diversity in my school.	5.2.4 Maintain staff awareness of the main orientations and general objectives regarding student achievement.
Method:	
5.1.4 Organize my time to make teacher supervision a priority.	**Method:**
5.1.5 Supervise the attainment of the achievement objectives.	5.2.5 Objectively analyze the school's climate.
5.1.6 Encourage and support the pedagogical projects of my teachers and assist them in their professional development related to the school's priorities and the students' needs.	5.2.6 Develop and implement a pluriannual supervision plan for my teachers.
	5.2.7 Use data collection and analysis tools.
	5.2.8 Agree to the mutual expectations during the individual/group supervision process.
5.1.7 Supervise the compliance to national/local policies and those of the school in matters of pedagogy.	5.2.9 Guide each supervised teacher to self-evaluate and set professional growth objectives.
5.1.8 Financially support my teachers' pedagogical projects and professional development needs.	5.2.10 Provide constructive individual/group feedback following supervision activities and follow up accordingly.
5.1.9 Structure organization to enable teachers to attend professional development activities.	
5.1.10 Perform teacher supervision with no subjectivity.	

(Continued)

Table 3.1. *(Continued)*

Pedagogically	In Human Relations
Cooperation: 5.1.11 Establish work groups/PLCs in my school and encourage peer collaboration. 5.1.12 Assist my school-team in finding and applying the most effective educational practices for the specific needs of the students.	**Cooperation:** 5.2.11 Consult school district services for specific expertise. **Communication:** 5.2.12 Communicate clearly with my teachers. **Ethics:** 5.2.13 Encourage and organize development activities based on the school's needs and those of the teachers. 5.2.14 Use differentiated supervision for behaviors related to the motivation, commitment, and professional competence of the supervised teacher. 5.2.15 Ensure that the rules of confidentiality are respected. 5.2.16 Acknowledge the personal/collective contributions and successes of my teachers. 5.2.17 Demonstrate managerial courage in certain supervision situations. 5.2.18 Declare my intentions and explain my supervision actions.
Know How to Be	
Pedagogically	*In Human Relations*
Ethics: 6.1.1 Be consistent in my educational values and my professional practice. 6.1.2 Welcome pedagogical initiatives.	**Method:** 6.2.1 Be flexible and available. **Cooperation:** 6.2.2 Be sociable. **Ethics:** 6.2.3 Be fair. 6.2.4 Believe in the progress and professional development of each supervised person. **Emotional intelligence:** 6.2.5 Possess a strong sense of personal efficacy. 6.2.6 Manage my stress and emotions. 6.2.7 Consider the emotional and affective dimension of the supervised person and show empathy. 6.2.8 Be a good listener. 6.2.9 Make people comfortable and trusting.

Know How to Become	
Pedagogically	*In Human Relations*
7.1.1 Self-evaluate and identify my training needs in pedagogy and supervision. 7.1.2 Learn more about pedagogical innovations and winning trends in this field. 7.1.3 Develop my professional development program in pedagogy. 7.1.4 Keep abreast of new theories and practices in teacher supervision	7.2.1 Learn more about human relations approaches.

Part II

COMPETENCY STANDARDS FRAMEWORK

Chapter Four

The Knowledge for Effective Supervision

If we understand that theoretical, contextual, and procedural knowledge helps us to grasp, describe, and explain an object or a situation and to propose action, the supervisor can thus be considered as someone who possesses the necessary skills to perform and consolidate the supervision process.

4.1—PEDAGOGICAL KNOWLEDGE

In this section, we examine five pedagogical skills:

- have a pedagogical vision and educational values;
- know the national and local policies pertaining to teacher supervision;
- know my school's issues regarding student achievement;
- know the resources provided by education services to support my teacher supervision practice; and
- know the basic principles of pedagogical supervision.

4.1.1—Have a Pedagogical Vision and Educational Values

The supervisor is first and foremost an educator who has teaching experience and is trained in pedagogy. While this training and experience provide the basic competencies, other skills are also necessary to successfully perform these functions.

The supervisor must be a model who demonstrates the school's vision; they must promote and target the creation of meaning for the members of their school-team. The successful supervisor understands their pedagogical role: they know when to intervene with teachers to help improve their teaching practices, they provide professional support where needed, and they acknowledge the quality of their teachers' efforts (Lapointe & Archambault, 2013). In fact, pedagogical knowledge should be as important for administrators as it is for teachers (Marzano, Waters, & McNulty, 2016). The effective supervisor also recognizes the importance of focusing their administrative decisions on student achievement. To do so, they are guided by a transparent system of values that they express to teachers through their interest in pedagogy and a vision that is apparent in every administrative decision they make.

Moreover, the school leader/teaching supervisor is often the person responsible for the introduction of reforms within their school. This mandate requires a level of balance between external prerogatives and the supervisor's personal views (Derrington, 2016). Indeed, Knapp and Feldman (2012) referred to the struggle that takes place during the construction of a pedagogical vision as a "marriage" between external and internal expectations.

4.1.2—Know the National and Local Policies Pertaining to Teacher Supervision

The supervisor must know the legal considerations governing their role and ideally master these aspects in order to be able to protect themselves and exercise their role more effectively. Understanding the inherent legalities also favors a respect of the supervised members' rights. Indeed, according to Ribas (2005), the supervisor who acquires and understands this knowledge of policy before beginning to supervise is better prepared to deal with any potential doubts or conflicts. A principal who does not fully grasp this knowledge will be unable to adequately reinvest it within the various contexts of their practice.

The supervisor must first be aware of the main orientations of the national Department of Education regarding teacher supervision, which may include legislation pertaining to pedagogical management. In addition, the supervisor must be well versed in curricula, teaching, and evaluation (Dupuis, 2004). Furthermore, to provide truly effective supervision, their knowledge of education programs must be up to date (Bernatchez, 2011; Boutet & Rousseau, 2002).

The successful supervisor is also aware of the pedagogical frameworks regulating each academic level in their school, the government policies relative to teacher supervision, the annual reforms, and last but not least, the broad lines of the collective agreements of both their teaching and nonteaching personnel. Locally, they keep abreast of their district's broad orientations and policies with regard to pedagogical supervision.

Finally, every good supervisor oversees the implementation of their school's main orientations, policy objectives, rules, and procedures.

4.1.3—Know the School's Issues Regarding Student Achievement

Every pedagogical supervisor should understand their school's specific characteristics. This information is acquired from official as well as unofficial sources. Official sources may include, among others, school performance data (student outcomes), teacher movement statistics, the deprivation index, and such socioeconomic indicators as the mother's education level and the parents' employment status, while unofficial or informal sources often include discussions with the different members of the school team, with students, and with parents. A good supervisor understands that this information remains fragile, as it may potentially perpetuate prejudice; it is thus important that the supervisor sift through multiple-source information to obtain a clear picture of the reality of a person, a group, or a situation.

4.1.4—Know the Resources Provided by Education Services to Support My Teacher Supervision Practice

Supervisors cannot be experts on every education program; it is thus necessary at times to rely on other sources of expertise, such as that of their teachers and their district's education services.

The effective principal welcomes external support when needed. The teachers' reciprocity and rich experience and the district's expert resources thus converge to improve student performances (Guillemette, 2011). The knowledge contributed can therefore be multi-sourced, involving such specialists as education consultants, learning specialists, psychologists, psychoeducators, and special education practitioners, to name a few (Guillemette, Morin, & Simon, 2015).

In many areas, education consultants are present to accompany teachers and school leaders. Houle and Pratte (2003) defined the roles, responsibilities, and skills of the education consultant as follows:

1. Enhance the teachers' expertise in pedagogy and in their disciplinary field.
2. Serve as an individual or group pedagogical consultant for both teachers and principals.
3. Use my pedagogical resources to serve the school.
4. Contribute to the development of pedagogy and related concerns.
5. Counsel new teachers to help them adapt to their new functions.
6. Counsel teachers regarding their professional development.
7. Contribute to the development of education programs (elaboration, implementation, evaluation).
8. Act as pedagogical leader (convey orientations, propose innovative projects, counsel teachers).
9. Contribute to school development by assisting principals and their teachers (student achievement project, thematic activity weeks, educational initiatives, etc.).
10. Respond to the support needs of the teachers and their principals.
11. Organize training activities for teachers and their principals.
12. Counsel teachers on which didactic materials to use.
13. Promote collaborations between schools.

4.1.5—Know the Basic Principles of Pedagogical Supervision

It is crucial that supervisors develop their vision of sustainable pedagogical supervision. Elaborating this vision is relevant in many aspects when it contributes to:

- establishing credibility, pedagogical leadership, and the deployment of relevant and coherent actions;
- giving meaning to their strategies and subsequent actions; and

- understanding, analyzing, and structuring supervision to attain goals and make adjustments when necessary.

In other words, it is maintaining the focus on academic achievement by adding pedagogical supervision while considering the various contextual factors involved (school-related factors: human and material resources; non-school-related factors: environmental characteristics, those of the family).

Every teacher has their own history with supervision or has an idea based on the experiences of their peers. When first entering the profession, the teacher is "evaluated," in the true sense of the word: they are exposed to a hierarchical relationship, where important decisions are made regarding their career. Consequently, this situation influences their perception of supervision, which stays with them throughout their career. Therefore, before asking the person being supervised to explain their vision, the supervisor must first clarify their own.

It is necessary that principals fully grasp the whys and wherefores of the concept of teacher supervision to ensure the sustained professional development of each teacher and to reach the objectives of the school's annual priorities.

In this perspective, the successful supervisor understands:

- the steps of good pedagogical management, namely, *analyzing* the situation, *planning* and *implementing* pedagogical actions with the teachers, and subsequently *regulating* these actions in regards to the students' academic success (Guillemette, Morin, & Simon, 2015);
- what pedagogical supervision (individual or collective) truly is (cf. chapter 2) and how it differs from the concept of evaluation. Teacher *supervision* is an organizational function associated with the guidance and professional development of the teacher. Its goal is improving teaching practices and, ultimately, student outcomes. *Evaluation*, on the other hand, is an organizational function that focuses on formulating an opinion or judgment regarding the teacher's performance and acquisition of skills (Nolan & Hoover, 2008); and
- the different types of pedagogical supervision (individual or collective).

Supervision must target the needs of the teachers being supervised by taking into account their sociocognitive, socioprofessional, and socioaffective characteristics and those of their school to ultimately support them in their professional development throughout their career (Zepeda, 2006). Table 4.1 presents several types of supervision based on the studies of Bouchamma (2005; 2006) and others.

Understanding these models enables the supervisor to deploy different strategies to address the lack of time to ensure supervision, and to call on the capabilities of their peers when lacking certain skills. This of course requires two things: knowing their own style of leadership and knowing their staff well, which in fact provides supervisors with better options to choose from (Bouchamma, 2004). Moreover, research shows that supervision that works is differentiated to suit each supervised teacher (Bouchamma, 2007).

Table 4.1. Types of Supervision Models

Supervision Models	Description
Traditional	• This model is used by schools who want their teaching to be uniform. • Supervision is considered a teaching action. The supervisor is viewed as the expert, while teachers have the role of executors. • The supervisor helps the teacher to acquire the necessary skill set to apply the program and meet the needs of the system.
Clinical	• This model is associated with counselling and therapy methods. • A form of partnership between supervisor and teacher based on individual needs, with intervention centered on the teacher's in-class behavior.

Self-supervision	• The portfolio is a tool that may be used in self-supervision, whether individually, by a group, or by the school (Gordon, 2016), through discussion and research via reflection, analysis, and sharing among colleagues. It may contain references, professional documentation, and practical suggestions.
	• Self-supervision may take place using different approaches (Glickman, Gordon, & Ross-Gordon, 2013):
	  ◦ *Controlled directive approach*: Used with supervised teachers who have less expertise, who participate less, or who show little interest in a pedagogical problem that must be dealt with rapidly.
	  ◦ *Informal directive approach*: Encourages supervised teachers to consider/choose alternative pedagogical actions.
	  ◦ *Collaborative approach*: Encourages colleagues to participate in decision making; favors the elaboration and development of action plans shared between the supervisor and their supervised teachers.
	  ◦ *Non-directive approach*: Supports the supervised teacher who wishes to establish their own action plan. This approach calls for reflection, attentiveness, and encouragements, as well as results analysis/problem-solving strategies.

Differentiated	• This model takes into account that supervised teachers have different needs in terms of their pedagogical practices, professional growth, and supervision preferences. • This model also considers the sociocognitive, socioprofessional, and socioaffective characteristics of the teachers and those of their school and supports their professional development throughout their career (Zepeda, 2006).
By peers	• Teachers work in pairs, share feedback, and discuss their teaching practices based on observations (Acheson & Gall, 2003; Nolan & Hoover, 2004). • Supervision is more collegial than conventional (Glickman, Gordon, & Ross-Gordon, 2014), which constitutes a crucial aspect of pedagogical leadership (Drago-Severson, 2012; Drago-Severson & Blum DeStefano, 2016). • This model centers on dialogue between teachers and the sharing of practices. The teacher's voice and experience are important to improve both teaching and learning (Wilhelm, 2013).

(Continued)

Table 4.1. *(Continued)*

Supervision Models	Description

By peers	• There are several types of peer supervision:
	  ◦ Mentoring. The mentor guides, protects, and helps the teacher to develop their skills in a climate of trust. Mentoring dyads are composed of a mentor (generally a veteran teacher or one who has exceptional pedagogical and relational skills) and a mentoree (generally a teacher beginning their career or one with specific needs) (Sergiovanni & Starratt, 2006).
	  ◦ Learning communities, professional learning communities, and communities of practice (Dionne, Lemyre, & Savoie-Zajc, 2010; Bouchamma, April, & Basque, 2017).

Research-action	• In this model, a teacher or group of teachers formally agrees to examine their teaching practices and work on solutions for improvement (Nolan & Hoover, 2004; Sergiovanni & Starratt, 2006).
	• This model enables teachers to develop their reflection toward their pedagogy and enhance their problem-solving abilities.
	• The questions raised by the teachers may pertain to students, teaching, teachers, curriculum, and school organization (Nolan & Hoover, 2004).
	• This is a four-tiered process:
	  ◦ Identify the problem (finding a subject of research, initial questions, action plan).
	  ◦ Collect the data (primary sources: questionnaires and observations; secondary sources: portfolios and reports).
	  ◦ Analyze the data.
	  ◦ Take action.
	• According to Nolan and Hoover (2004), the teacher who begins a research action must:
	  ◦ Actively invest in their own development, on an issue they believe is relevant, by collaborating with other professionals;
	  ◦ Be documented, take courses, get training, go to workshops;
	  ◦ Be prepared to take risks and try new approaches;
	  ◦ Use a critical eye to validate the correlation between the measures established to solve a problem and its impact in the classroom.

Winning teacher supervision practices that are supported by research must be adopted because they offer a perspective that complements practical knowledge, which in turn equips teachers to better deal with issues in their practice. To this effect, Bouchamma, Giguère, and April (2016) identified the most successful teacher supervision practices retained in the literature:

- Identify priorities.
- Clearly communicate to my staff the definition of pedagogical supervision (individual and collective) and the objectives to be established.
- Begin my individual program with volunteers.
- Be transparent, coherent, and fair throughout the process.
- Start with data, facts, and observations.
- Apply each step of the administrative process.

- Establish facilitating structures (professional development opportunities for the staff, provisions for financial and material resources, etc.) to perform my supervision.
- Involve my staff in the process through my teacher participation committee or other groups (pedagogical innovation committee, pedagogical facilitation committee, etc.).
- Set up professional practice communities.
- Use the individual/collective sense of efficacy of my staff as the starting point for my supervision.
- Establish networks for the sharing of practices.
- The leadership styles for effective teacher supervision are: pedagogical, transformational, relational, situational, ethical, and shared. According to Arpin and Capra (2008), appropriating these different conceptual elements of pedagogical supervision thus makes it possible to refresh and update one's frame of reference (representations, beliefs, values), to adjust interventions, and to progress in the role of facilitator.
- Supervision is not limited to individual practice.

Hallinger (2005) showed the importance of instilling in the minds of school leaders the concept of the learning community, which represents a positive and sustainable action for schools.

4.2—KNOWLEDGE IN HUMAN RELATIONS

In this section, we examine five areas of knowledge in human relations:

- Know the organizational culture and particularities of the work environment.
- Know the personal and professional profile of each supervised teacher.
- Know my leadership and management styles.
- Know the services provided by human resources to support my teacher supervision practice.
- Know facilitation techniques.

4.2.1—Know the Organizational Culture and Particularities of the Work Environment

An organizational culture represents all of the common attitudes, values, and beliefs that guide the behavior of the members within an organization (Schermerhorn, Hunt, Osborn, & de Billy, 2014). In other words, it is a "group's individual and collective ways of thinking, believing, and knowing, which includes their shared experiences, consciousness, skills, values, forms of expression, social institutions and behaviors" (Tillman, 2002, p. 4). According to Glanz and Zepeda (2015), this culture also includes the values, traditions, communication, learning styles, contributions, and relational models and that it is "dynamic, multifaceted, embedded in context, socially constructed, learned, and dialectical" (Nieto, 1999, in Glanz & Zepeda, 2015).

Supervisors can influence how their supervised teachers develop their own perceptions, values, and beliefs regarding the organization, learning, and teaching.

Furthermore, similar to the school culture, which develops over time, social and cultural norms also come to influence school climate (Witherspoon Arnold, 2016).

Leaders who take their organization's culture and its members into account have strong beliefs and attitudes, have a sound understanding of groups, and possess significant relational expertise (Glanz & Zepeda, 2015).

The influence the supervisor has on student learning is thus transmitted through several channels, including the school's culture and climate (Hallinger & Heck, 1998), which is why it is important to create a culture that nurtures teaching and learning (Fink & Resnick, 2001), because without it, academic success is comprised (Watson, 2001).

Each school has its own characteristics, its own system of beliefs, values, and standards that shape the daily lives of teachers and is the result of tradition and practice. Past experiences teachers may have had with supervision will also mold the supervisor's approach, hence the importance of identifying and comprehending the school's culture before introducing any new processes (Leithwood et al., 2008). Understanding this culture and the related characteristics is key in the current context of an education system affected by so many reforms and changes (Pelletier, 2006).

In addition to understanding the organizational culture, the effective leader must also be aware of the union culture in regards to teacher supervision to better adapt their interventions and actions. Indeed, how the system works, its specifics, and the cultural and pedagogical realities of the school are all aspects that help the supervisor to respond better to expectations and to adapt their practices to the path and profile of their supervised teachers (Arpin & Capra, 2008).

4.2.2—Know the Personal and Professional Profile of Each Supervised Teacher

Teachers have a variety of preferences with regard to the type of aid they envisage during their supervision (Bouchamma, 2007). It is therefore imperative that supervisors know their supervised teachers and their history so that the process is personalized (Zepeda, 2006). They must consider their teachers' past and present, their future aspirations, their challenges, their worries, their level of knowledge and development, their strengths and weaknesses, their degree of professional maturity and commitment, and their level of professional competence (Pelletier, 2006; Rousseau, 2005). For example, the professional development needs of tenured faculty differ from those of new teachers.

The level of teacher investment and motivation may be determined by such indicators as the willingness to take on responsibilities, the desire to succeed at a given task, the level of involvement, the amount of initiative and autonomy, their tenacity, and finally, their level of flexibility. The level of professional expertise regarding the tasks involved is likely to be explained by teaching experience; the knowledge, level of comprehension, and requirements of the designated task; the ability to take on responsibilities and meet deadlines; work efficacy; and the ability to solve problems (Pelletier, 2006).

As a result, the proposed supervision may take on different forms depending on the teachers' profiles. It may be more formal, or more or less supportive; it may include peer sponsorship, adapted training, greater reinforcement or delegation, and so on (Lauzon & Madgin, 2003).

To provide effective supervision, the supervisor must initially, and whenever possible, know the profile of the teacher they are to supervise, particularly new, incoming teachers they do not know. Perhaps the supervisor is the new arrival in the school, hence the importance of knowing your teachers prior to beginning their supervision. Here, the professional portfolio is a very insightful tool for the supervisor to fully understand their teacher's profile. This professional profile should ideally contain the following elements:

- On a personal level:
  - their main qualities: jovial, rational, punctual, and so on;
  - their principal areas for improvement: impulsiveness, shyness, and so on;
  - their favorite hobbies or interests; and
  - others.
- Their education:
  - their basic training; and
  - any professional development activities/training.
- Their professional experience in teaching and in others
- Their professional competence

As regards the teachers' professional competencies, the supervisor will require data obtained through either their observations, their previous discussions with the supervised teacher, or existing data, such as student outcomes, and so on. These data are obviously useful for the first interview with a teacher the supervisor does not know, and for subsequent meetings this profile will be an excellent reference tool.

4.2.3—Know My Leadership and Management Styles

According to Cormier (2002), self-knowledge teaches us to reflect on ourselves with grace and humor, admit our mistakes, and deal with situations with a certain level of objectivity. The ability of school leaders to self-manage and to learn about themselves is therefore recommended to promote a climate that nurtures learning.

The successful supervisor knows their management style, whether it be directive, consultative, or participative. It goes without saying that the consultative style, and, in particular, the participative style, helps build a strong relationship between supervisor and supervised teacher. These management styles can be more or less controlled.

These leaders must also be able to determine which leadership style is the most appropriate to use with the supervised teacher: situational, transactional, transformational, pedagogical, ethical, shared, relational, or collaborative. According to Legendre (2005), a leadership style is a personal way to exercise this authority. The styles most mentioned in the literature are autocratic, authoritative or paternalistic, participative, and democratic. Several factors determine the leadership style; these may include the leader's personality and values, the teachers' abilities, interests, level of maturity and instruction, the physical environment, the nature of the problem involved, time

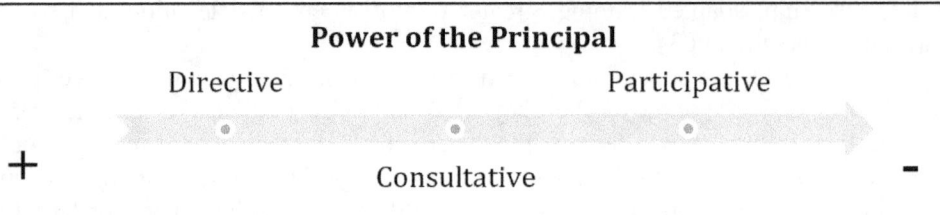

Figure 4.1. Management Styles from Most to Least Controlling
Original figure created by the authors

availability, technology, and the relationship between the supervisor and the supervised teacher (Legendre, 2005).

Studies abound on the subject of school leadership, along with an increasing variety of concepts, which adds an element of complexity to this field. Table 4.2 presents a synthesis of the main styles of leadership.

Because no approach is successful in every circumstance, the supervisor's management and leadership styles must be constantly adapted for each teacher and each situation.

4.2.4—Know the Services Provided by Human Resources to Support My Teacher Supervision Practice

Supervisors are not specialists in the application of collective agreements, which is why they must at times call on the human resources services of their district. These services are provided, among others, to support supervisors in their evaluation of nontenured faculty, teachers in difficulty, or difficult teachers.

4.2.5—Know Facilitation Techniques

Pedagogical facilitation is an invaluable skill every good supervisor should have (Dupuis, 2004). Acheson and Gall (2003) described seven facilitation techniques in pedagogical supervision:

1. Listen more, talk less: It is difficult to consider the preoccupations of the supervised teacher during a conversation or to encourage their plans for improvement when you do all the talking.
2. Acknowledge, paraphrase, and repeat what the teacher has said; accurate reformulation indicates to them that you are listening.
3. Ask for clarification: To avoid bad communication, ask questions such as "What do you mean by . . . ?" or "Tell me more about. . . ."
4. Recognize and applaud the teacher's development and efforts: highlight instances when the teacher has shown growth and effectiveness regarding a particular objective.

5. Avoid giving direct warnings right away: wait until the teacher has had time to process and interpret a situation before giving any directives (this also helps improve their level of autonomy).
6. Provide verbal support: help the teacher identify their professional objectives in regards to student achievement. You need their feedback before helping them reach the determined objectives.
7. Acknowledge and use what the teacher is feeling: consider the emotional content in what they are saying.

When ensuring supervision with a group of teachers, a good supervisor:

- encourages the sharing of practices;
- establishes a climate that supports teamwork;
- develops a common language within the group;
- determines with the school-team how the meetings will be conducted;
- favors collective decision making;
- repeats the established orientations to the members; and
- summarizes the information.

Table 4.2. Synthesis of the Main Knowledge for Effective Supervision

Pedagogical Skills	*Human Relations Skills*
4.1.1 Have a pedagogical vision and educational values.	4.2.1 Know the organizational culture and particularities of the work environment.
4.1.2 Know the national and local policies pertaining to teacher supervision.	4.2.2 Know the personal and professional profile of each supervised teacher.
4.1.3 Know my school's issues regarding student achievement.	4.2.3 Know my leadership and management styles.
4.1.4 Know the resources provided by education services to support my teacher supervision practice.	4.2.4 Know the services provided by human resources to support my teacher supervision practice.
4.1.5 Know the basic principles of pedagogical supervision.	4.2.5 Know facilitation techniques.

Chapter Five

The *Know How to Do* Every Supervisor Should Possess

Knowing how to do refers to the skills that are necessary to perform a given task. These operational capabilities are defined as the aptitude a person has to successfully perform a physical, intellectual, or professional activity (Legendre, 2005). This competence is either acquired or developed by the supervisor.

5.1—PEDAGOGICAL *KNOW HOW TO DO*

In this section, 12 pedagogical *know how to do* pertaining to the orders of leadership (3), method (7), and cooperation (2) are examined:

- Use pedagogical leadership: promote my vision of the school system, my educational orientations and values; encourage the professional development of my staff; support pedagogical projects and innovation.
- Use situational leadership: focus on the students' needs and the school's education priorities.
- Manage ethnocultural diversity in my school.
- Organize my time to make teacher supervision a priority.
- Supervise the attainment of the achievement objectives.
- Encourage and support the pedagogical projects of my teachers and assist them in their professional development related to the school's priorities and the students' needs.
- Supervise the compliance to national/local policies and those of the school in matters of pedagogy.
- Financially support my teachers' pedagogical projects and professional development needs.
- Structure organization to enable teachers to attend professional development activities.
- Perform teacher supervision with no subjectivity.
- Establish work groups/PLCs in my school and encourage peer collaboration.
- Assist my school-team in finding and applying the most effective educational practices for the specific needs of the students.

Pedagogical Leadership

5.1.1—Use Pedagogical Leadership: Promote My Vision of the School System, My Educational Orientations and Values; Encourage the Pedagogical Development of My Staff; Support Pedagogical Projects and Innovation

A good supervisor exercises pedagogical leadership by focusing their actions on teaching and learning, setting high achievement standards, implementing education programs, monitoring student progress, and supervising the pedagogical actions of their teachers (Marks & Printy, 2003; Sergiovanni & Starratt, 2006).

The supervisor who uses pedagogical leadership stimulates their teachers' interest in these pedagogical actions in relation to student outcomes (Collerette, Pelletier, & Turcotte, 2013). This leader also takes on the role of agent of change by protecting teachers who take risks (Marzano, Waters, & McNulty, 2016).

According to Archambault and Richer (2007), being an agent of change represents a serious investment, with actions that mobilize the school-team on aspects that improve student learning. The supervision of pedagogical practices is a strong mobilization tool used by the supervisor to communicate their vision to help their teachers reflect on their practices and to support them in their professional growth.

All things considered, the most important duty of the supervisor is to promote the lifelong development of learning skills (research, reflection, collaboration, and professional development) (Zepeda, 2012).

5.1.2—Use Situational Leadership: Focus on the Students' Needs and the School's Education Priorities

In our examination of the various leadership theories, situational leadership highlights the importance of considering and responding to factors related to context and its particularities (Bass & Stogdill, 1990; Leithwood, Leithwood, & Daniel, 1998). In this theory, situational characteristics associated with the traits and behaviors of the leader make it possible to predict the performance of a given leadership (Schermerhorn, Hunt, Osborn, & de Billy, 2014). In fact, how the school leader reacts when responding to the different situations they encounter may vary depending on the nature and preferences of the staff, the work conditions, and the tasks to be performed (Northouse, 2007).

5.1.3—Manage Ethnocultural Diversity in My School

Society expects that school-teams adapt to the ethnocultural diversity in their schools (Witherspoon Arnold, 2016). Supervisors thus have the responsibility of promoting equitable education, implementing pedagogical practices that support this diversity (Gardiner & Enomoto, 2006), and motivating their teams to overcome challenges in this regard (Kiemele, 2009).

The effective supervisor demonstrates a profound understanding of the school culture and that of the individuals within its walls (Leithwood & Jantzi, 2000; Witherspoon Arnold, 2016). They must therefore strive to create an environment that is respectful and attentive to every voice (Witherspoon Arnold, 2016) and always defend beliefs and values that encourage greater student achievement to ultimately establish a school climate that favors the growth of both the students and their teachers (Glanz, 2006). Effectively managing ethnocultural diversity thus enables school leaders to create opportunities that nurture the exchange of ideas, innovativeness, and creativity.

To achieve this, the supervisor or "cultural mediator" (Jay, 2003; Witherspoon Arnold, 2016) encourages the teachers to adopt educational approaches that are based on the knowledge and skills students demonstrate in class. Indeed, the daily efforts of the latter are known to increase when they feel competent. The supervisor must also ensure that their teachers are properly trained to mediate cultural differences and contexts (Witherspoon Arnold, 2016). This mediation may be in the form of collaborative actions and interpersonal relationships with persons of other countries, inclusion practices in the classroom, translation, and intercultural learning (Gercek, 2008; Witherspoon Arnold, 2016).

To actually favor cultural contingency and a culturally adapted supervision relationship, the supervisor must look at the cultural background of each person. Discussing mutual expectations in a supervision process is a way to better understand the culture of the teachers and their students and the inherent nuances that may influence teachers' perceptions. A supervisor who is culturally reactive transfers this accountability to their supervised teachers, who in turn are empowered to develop their own leadership skills in this regard. Moreover, to support this culturally adapted supervision, Pack-Brown, Thomas, and Seymour (2008) proposed that supervisors favor humility over authority in their approach. Finally, a supervisor who acknowledges diversity promotes diversity, conducts self-evaluations, arbitrates differences, adapts to the cultural realities of the communities they serve, and allocates resources toward cultural acceptance (Levin & Fullan, 2008; Witherspoon Arnold, 2016).

Effective management of diversity is crucial in light of the many challenges this entails for the supervisor: the lack of awareness regarding the culture of immigrant students, the possible personal prejudice, discrimination and racism (Gardiner & Enomoto, 2006; McGlynn, 2009), the lack of differentiated pedagogy and curricula (Dejaeghere & Zhang, 2008; Frawley & Fasoli, 2012), and the lack of adequate didactic material and other resources (Kanouté et al., 2008).

Finally, research reveals a lack of specific programs on the preparation of principals and their teachers to deploy effective actions in multiethnic contexts. Indeed, the head supervisor is a cultural leader (Glanz, 2006) and must therefore contribute to the skills development of their school-team in this regard. In this perspective, teacher supervision is an opportunity to train staff on issues related to diversity management (Hajisoteriou, 2012). In some areas, other measures may be used, such as providing the assistance of a liaison officer (a professional whose responsibility is to identify ways to connect the needs of the students and their community and those of the teachers). Overall, supervisors must adopt an open-minded attitude, whereby every student and teacher has value and deserves to be encouraged (Heckman-Stone, 2003) and guided with dignity throughout the entire supervision process (Witherspoon Arnold, 2016).

Method

5.1.4 — Organize My Time to Make Teacher Supervision a Priority

Even with the best of intentions and the necessary skills to provide teachers with individual/group supervision to improve their teaching practices, some supervisors often have difficulty completing their supervision process. This is generally explained by the time spent on duties that are unrelated to pedagogy. Indeed, Zepeda (2016) has reported several studies showing that school leaders do not spend enough time on pedagogical issues and too much time on other tasks.

As a result, the challenge of satisfying teachers' educational needs has generated increased interest in the commitment to and development of peer expertise. This supervision by peers takes place in either formal or informal contexts through differentiated leadership and collegial supervision (Klar et al., 2016).

It is thus of the utmost importance that teachers have autonomy in their practices, as this gives the supervisor more time to attend to their other duties. Teacher supervision is thus an excellent approach to render teachers professionally accountable, once the process has ended.

According to Archambault and Garon (2012), to perform effective teacher supervision, time must be set aside to attend one's own professional meetings and continuing education, to actively participate in training activities held in the school, to brainstorm with the education consultant, to keep abreast of pedagogical reforms, and to share one's discoveries with the school-team by making documentation available in the staff lounge and proposing articles of pedagogical interest in a weekly newsletter.

To remedy the issue of lack of time, a good supervisor must, for example, use supervision models that involve other actors (mentoring, self-supervision using the portfolio, learning and practice communities, etc.). In addition, their actions must have an order or priority in contexts of individual supervision (Bouchamma, Giguère, & April, 2016):

1. Supervising nontenured faculty and those in difficulty: only in these two instances should supervision lead to an evaluation. In this case, it is important that the supervisor clearly explains the objectives of the supervision with the concerned;
2. Supervising newly hired teachers who are new to the school;
3. Establishing pluriannual priorities for the other teachers;
4. Recognizing teachers who have excelled in their work during the year with a short ceremony, if you have not had the time to meet with them in your regular duties.

5.1.5 — Supervise the Attainment of the Achievement Objectives

The supervisor must make sure there is consistency between the school's orientations and objectives, the actions of their school-team, and the legal policies governing the practice. To this effect, Brassard (2009) put forth that the effective supervisor incites their staff to adopt the national project and determine a measure that will satisfy both clientele/staff expectations and their needs/characteristics. These actions must of course comply with the prescribed education program as well as national and intermediate legislation.

Ultimately, the supervisor is accountable. They must look at the results on a daily basis throughout the process and proceed with the necessary adjustments when warranted.

Formulating My Objectives

Determining an objective is an important step. We recommend the SMART system to formulate your objectives.

Formulating a SMART Objective

Many factors favor the elaboration of objectives, through which the obtained results can be evaluated. In addition to clarifying the direction to take and coordinating various activities, these factors make it possible to create a connection between the members responsible for the attainment of these objectives, which ultimately encourages *motivation* and *commitment*. Indeed, whether individual or collective, each supervision process must be based on clear and measurable objectives, realistic deadlines, and significant regulation methods.

When it comes to formulating work objectives with teachers (either individually, in a PLC [professional learning community], or with committees), it is recommended that the supervisor prepare by using the following SMART criteria, namely, *Specific*, *Measurable*, *Attainable*, *Realistic*, and *Temporal*. These criteria require the identification of performance indicators and make it possible to establish objectives with measurable descriptions of what the supervised teacher is supposed to achieve during the exercise.

Performance indicators describe how an observer can determine whether the results have been obtained. These results may be qualitative, quantitative, or a combination of both. The supervisor must define the scaffold for the expected level of achievement and determine the dates of completion.

- **S: Specific.** The objective for improvement clearly explains the expectations. It describes an observable measure or an achievement. It also defines the result rather than the actual process.
- **M: Measurable.** A method or procedure exists to evaluate and describe the result in terms of units (quality, quantity, cost, time, etc.). Some results are easily measurable, while others must be verified or observed.
- **A: Attainable.** The work objective is realistic and achievable. The best objectives are those that challenge the employees, without going to extremes. In other words, the objectives are not impossible to attain, nor are they lower that performance standards. Objectives that are too big or too small lose all significance and thus fail to motivate.
- **R: Realistic.** The objective corresponds to the role the employee plays in their workplace.
- **T: Temporal.** The objective falls within a determined period of time.

5.1.6 — Encourage and Support the Pedagogical Projects of My Teachers and Assist Them in Their Professional Development Related to the School's Priorities and the Students' Needs

In collective professional development, teachers develop professionally in different ways. For example, teachers who have acquired skills in a specific strategy may facilitate workshops for their colleagues, some may propose demonstrations in their class, and others may propose that a team teach a specific lesson to a colleague in need.

Professional development must go beyond simple training. Supervisors must inform their teachers regarding new skills and the best methods to apply these skills. They must encourage their teachers to invest in personal reflection as well as reflective dialogue with the other pedagogical aspects (Gordon, 2016).

In their competency standard for school principals, Boyer, Corriveau, and Pelletier (2011) identified four components:

1. Exercise strategic leadership based on a shared vision.
2. Manage the school in an effective, proactive, and participative manner.
3. Mobilize the staff to achieve the school's mission.
4. Ensure educational and pedagogical development for the success of all parties concerned.

Regarding the final skill related to teacher supervision, the supervisor must be able to:

- establish strategies that favor continuous learning, the sharing of knowledge, individual and group reflection, and the development of education practices;
- support diversification and pedagogical differentiation, as well as the diversity and quality of the pedagogical approaches and methodologies;
- ensure the development of a learning evaluation system that is just and fair; and
- develop collaborations with different networks in the community toward student achievement.

To support the pedagogical projects of their teachers, supervisors should encourage their teachers to participate in professional development activities to learn more about problem-based learning, skills, and strategies, and how to transfer them into the classroom. As teachers integrate this new knowledge in class, their supervisor or their peers may schedule visits to cyclically gather observation data and discuss with them the best away to adapt their new teaching skills with their students (Gordon, 2016).

To summarize, the supervisor must support the professional growth of their teachers and encourage them to welcome change.

5.1.7 — Supervise the Compliance to National/Local Policies and Those of the School in Matters of Pedagogy

There are many national (Department of Education) and local policies (school board and school). Due to their abundance, they are difficult to remember and simultaneously supervise.

Supervise the Education Services

Education services include instruction services, as well as complementary and specific services for the students.

Supervise the Application of the Education Programs

Studies on successful schools show that supervisors in these schools focus their pedagogical supervision on the education programs, existing teaching strategies, and teaching practices (Heck, Larsen, & Marcoulides, 1990; Heck, Marcoulides, & Lang, 1991). Efforts should therefore go toward addressing these elements.

Supervise the Development of the Teachers' Skills

A good supervisor is one who provides their teachers with the necessary professional development opportunities that tangibly improve how they teach (Marzano, Waters, & McNulty, 2016). However, this leader must consider their teachers' acquired skills to better position them in their continuing development and to leave a door open for other growth opportunities down the road that will gradually add to their expertise.

That said, the availability of resources does not necessary mean that they are used. Indeed, some teachers simply refuse to be subjected to the proposed aid (they can accept or refuse), which can be a perplexing situation for some supervisors.

Professional development must first and foremost correspond to the teachers' needs so that they, in turn, are better prepared to respond to the needs of their students. To identify these needs, the effective supervisor uses tact, asks questions, encourages them, and may consider disciplinary measures as a last resort.

Supervise All of the Implementation Stages of a Pedagogical Reform

During the mobilization process to welcome change, the school leader must follow certain steps in a socioconstructivist approach toward this reform (Pastor & Bréard, 2004). The stages of this process are:

1. knowledge of the reform;
2. analysis of the situation within the organization;
3. development of an implementation plan with the other stakeholders;
4. implementation of the proposed actions;
5. supervision of the action plan; and
6. assessment of the reform's implementation.

Chin and Benne (1991) also suggested adding the co-construction of the reform with the persons who will experience this change. For these authors, implementing change fares better when it is done through collaborative actions.

5.1.8—Financially Support My Teachers' Pedagogical Projects and Professional Development Needs

As public funding is increasingly rare, it is necessary for today's schools to develop strategies to "do more with less." However, this principle is not always unanimous and must not be equated with doing less for the students (Levenson, 2011). The search for new ways to financially support schools has thus become a priority, in light of the slower economic growth affecting societies and the decrease in public funding for education (Tate, 2010).

In the context of economic growth, the Ministry or the Department of Education, depending on the education system, allocates funding based on specific priorities and asks its schools to develop projects according to these priorities.

5.1.9—Structure Organization to Enable Teachers to Attend Professional Development Activities

The importance of encouraging the professional development of teachers, despite the many different constraints, is constantly mentioned in the literature on school management. For example, Kaser, Mundry, Stiules, and Loucks-Horsley (2011) wrote that school leaders must support their teachers' motivation and commitment to learn by providing conducive conditions for this purpose, such as time and other structures and measures that favor learning.

One study on effective schools showed that one winning practice was to provide time for teachers to ensure a sharing of practices and professional development. When a supervisor brings in a supply teacher from time to time to free the teacher, this encourages the latter's reflection and helps them follow up on achieved objectives and work on those ahead. Another advantage is that it encourages discussion and strengthens the bond between administrators and teachers. Teachers are also permitted to attend training directly related to their practices and needs. Successful supervisors understand that teachers cannot get the proper training if they are not relieved of some of their duties to do so (Bouchamma, 2012).

5.1.10—Perform Teacher Supervision With No Subjectivity

During the supervision process, the supervisor will be called on to collect data in the classroom. Whether structured (using a grid) or not, the data collection through in-class observation must be exempt from possible biases and errors. The supervisor must be aware of what may alter their objectivity in the process. In this regard, Schermerhorn, Hunt, Osborn, and de Billy (2014) listed several biases; herein, the word *evaluation* may be replaced by the word *supervision* in the context of an individual approach.

- *Confirmation bias* (or trap): the highly common tendency to notice and remember only the information that supports our beliefs about something while at the same time failing to consider or remember information or events to the contrary.
- *Halo effect*: when an opinion of a person or situation is developed based on one attribute. For example, a teacher is perceived as being intelligent and trustworthy based solely on their good looks.

- *Contrast effect*: when the characteristics of a supervised teacher differ significantly from those of other supervised individuals met earlier and who were evaluated much more favorably or unfavorably by the supervisor.
- *Stereotype effect*: when the supervisor allows their personal prejudices regarding certain sociodemographic characteristics (such as ethnocultural origin, age, sex, sexual orientation, or handicap) to cloud their judgment.
- *Framing error*: a tendency to intervene by looking at only one angle of the situation. For example, the supervisor may risk an intervention if the problem is described in terms of loss, and less so if described in terms of success, even if the two sides provide the same information.
- *Representativeness*: a mental shortcut based on a few elements on which we have preconceived ideas that are not necessarily representative.
- *Weak differentiation error*: when the supervisor uses only one portion of an evaluation scale that more or less represents the whole. For example, on a scale from 1 to 10, from weak to excellent, the supervisor may fall prey to indulgence (tendency to score from 8 to 10), severity (from 1 to 5), or central tendency (from 6 to 8).
- *Availability bias*: when the supervisor, strongly influenced by recent events, tends to not consider past information that should be taken into account.

Zepeda (2016) observed that supervisors had a tendency to lack clarity in the methods and processes used to evaluate their teachers by using several data sources. Glanz and Zepeda (2015) wrote that the supervisor must have a solid database and avoid premature or hasty judgments. These data, in fact, enable supervisors and their supervised teachers to develop a common language when discussing practices. Finally, to avoid personal prejudices, the effective supervisor promotes awareness and understanding (Witherspoon Arnold, 2016).

Cooperation

5.1.11—Establish Work Groups/PLCs in My School and Encourage Peer Collaboration

Duffy (2016) argued that the control traditionally used in teacher supervision is inadequate because it centers on examining the behavior of each teacher by hypothesizing that if a sufficient number of teachers improved, so would teaching and learning. This author concluded that improving the education system called for a different, more collective approach.

An increasing number of recent studies on pedagogical leadership favor the adoption of collegial over individual supervision practices (Glickman, Gordon, & Ross-Gordon, 2014) as well as the benefits of collaboration on the development of school climate (Drago-Severson, Blum-DeStefano, & Asghar, 2013; Klar, Huggins, & Roessler, 2016).

The forms of collaboration may differ. According to Gable and Manning (1997), it may be direct (co-teaching or in-class observations) or indirect (common planning, development of action plans, etc.); indirect collaboration may be either horizontal (teachers in same level, the same discipline) or vertical (different levels, different disciplines).

In a school functioning as a PLC—or a professional learning community—the culture is always one of collaboration. Isolated teachers are embraced in a daily process of firmly anchored cooperation. Indeed, PLC members are not "invited" to work with their colleagues but are rather called on to contribute to a group effort focusing on helping all of the students to learn more effectively (Eaker, Dufour, & Dufour, 2004).

Several factors contribute to the implementation and sustainment of collaboration between teachers. These factors involve not only the teacher but also, by the same token, the supervisor's leadership and school-related factors (Bouchamma, Savoie, & Basque, 2012).

Teacher-Related Factors That Contribute to Sustaining Collaboration

1. The decision to participate or not in a collaborative team (Howden & Kopiec, 2002);
2. The importance of a common vision, values, and objectives (Kinkead, 2006; Saint-Germain, 2002) to be collectively responsible for a student (personal well-being and academic performance) (Holland, 2002; Shank, 2006);
3. The importance of respect, mutual trust (Howden & Kopiec, 2002; Shank, 2006; Tschannen-Moran, Uline, Woolfolk Hoy, & Mackley, 2000), and efficient communication (Pugach & Johnson, 1995);
4. The willingness to enter into group practice (Shank, 2006) through shared responsibilities and interdependency (Pugach & Johnson, 1995), equal contributions (Cook & Friend, 1993), and social skills and abilities (Coombs-Richardson & Rivers, 1998);
5. The willingness to improve (Riordan & Da Costa, 1996);
6. The enhancement of teamwork (Sergiovanni, 2001);
7. The need for equal status (Da Costa, 1995b) to collaborate on something other than that related to evaluation.

Leadership Factors That Contribute to Sustaining Collaboration

1. The supervisor's leadership: shared (Holland, 2002), adapted (Liontos, 1992), transformational (Kinkead, 2006; Lucas & Valentine, 2002; Marks & Printy, 2003), socioconstructivist (Saint-Germain, 2002), collaborative (Howden & Kopiec, 2002), pedagogical (Howden & Kopiec, 2002), and ethical (Langlois & Lapointe, 2002);
2. The supervisor's availability (Cook & Friend, 1993), the recognition of collaborative work (Inger, 1993a), the presentation of its benefits (Ogolla, 2003; Tschannen-Moran, Uline, Woolfolk Hoy, & Mackley, 2000), as well as the necessary training (Inger, 1993a; Newmann, 1994);
3. The supervisor's planning: temporal provisions (Eaker, Dufour, & Dufour, 2004), physical layout (Holland, 2002; Klonsky, 2002; Reed, 2003) and education policies (Inger, 1993b; Wang, Haertel, & Walberg, 1993), and the optimization of material resources (Inger, 1993a).

The Benefits of Collaboration

Collaboration produces positive effects on the student, the teacher, and the school staff as a whole. Indeed, teacher collaboration has a profound effect on the students by enabling them to experience academic success (Holland, 2002; Howden & Kopiec, 2002; Reed, 2003; Shank, 2006; Tschannen-Moran, Uline, Woolfolk Hoy, & Mackley, 2000) and collaborate better with other students (Holland, 2002; Howden & Kopiec, 2002) by influencing their attitudes and behaviors (Da Costa, 1993; 1995a) and promoting a greater sense of belonging (Reyes & Fuller, 1995). Teachers also benefit, as they are continuously learning and developing professionally (Spraker, 2003). It is through collaboration that teachers acquire *knowledge, know how to do, know how to be,* and *know how to become*:

1. *Knowledge*, thanks to collective reflection that enables them to evolve from *what* to *why* (Riordan & Da Costa, 1996);
2. *Know how to do*: practical educational know-how and pedagogical innovativeness (Al-Bataineh & Nur-Awaleh, 2000; Da Costa, 1993; 1995a; Riordan & Da Costa, 1996; Shank, 2006; Stevens, 1997);
3. *Know how to be*: no more isolation (Beeken, Shmidt, & Beaver, 1992; Da Costa, 1993; Inger, 1993a; Reyes & Fuller, 1995; Smith & Scott, 1990), lasting professional relationships based on trust and respect (Gable & Manning, 1997), daily enthusiasm, gratification, and satisfaction (Inger, 1993a), healthy interdependence (Riordan & Da Costa, 1996; Inger, 1993a), and leading by example (Tschannen-Moran, Uline, Woolfolk Hoy, & Mackley, 2000);
4. *Know how to become*: constant support and feedback from colleagues (Roberts & Pruitt, 2003) and non-hierarchical supervision (Da Costa, 1995a).

Finally, collaboration among teachers enables their school to become more effective and efficient (Éthier, 1989) because of the many benefits for

1. school climate and culture (Holland, 2002; Tschannen-Moran, Uline, Woolfolk Hoy, & Mackley, 2000);
2. school structure: adapted leadership (Liontos, 1992), shared leadership (Holland, 2002), shared supervision (Da Costa, 1995b), and better retention of personnel (Cook & Friend, 1993); and
3. its pedagogy.

Collaboration generally ensures better quality teaching (Inger, 1993a), a stronger acknowledgment of pedagogy and its role (Howden & Kopiec, 2002), and strong pedagogical innovation (Howden & Kopiec, 2002; Shank, 2006).

When work is performed collaboratively, it is possible for the supervisor to guide the group. This *collective* supervision is undertaken parallel to an individual supervision. Work groups and PLCs are the primary models in collective supervision. To attain their objectives, these groups may deploy several modalities, such as enquiries (questionnaires, surveys), existing data (analysis of student outcomes, stat grids, students' work), and contributions from experts.

The PLC is one mode of operation that fuels the collaborative efforts of the school-team and encourages members to collectively undertake activities and reflection to constantly improve student achievement (Roy & Hord, 2006).

The PLC thus represents a promising avenue in pedagogical supervision. Sharing experiences and winning practices indeed appears to be a particularly effective method that enables teachers to engage in the search for solutions as well as innovative actions and teaching practices.

The supervisor's leadership comes into play in a major way in the PLC approach by guiding the discussions, supporting and facilitating the sustainable integration of successful practices, and providing professional growth opportunities. Their role is therefore pivotal in the growth and energy level of PLCs. Leclerc (2010) put forth that a school that functions as a PLC gives meaning to the pedagogical interventions because teachers see the advantages of working in collaboration with peers on issues that concern them and that directly affect their interactions with their students. According to this author, the PLC actually *changes how they teach*. Indeed, this approach promotes the sharing of expertise among teachers and the integration of effective practices to meet the academic needs of their students. A culture of self-reliance is also evidenced, which brings creativity to the forefront and enhances their willingness to pursue their professional development (Leclerc, 2010).

Huffman and Hipp (2003) identified three development stages of a successful PLC, namely, initiation, implementation, and institutionalization. We have adapted the works of Huffman and Hipp (2003) and of Leclerc, Moreau, and Lépine (2009) to present a brief description of this organizational structure:

Stage 1: Initiation refers to the decision to proceed with experimentation in a PLC by introducing certain conditions (e.g., scheduled time to attend) to enable teachers to express their concerns regarding their students and practices and to share their winning strategies.

Stage 2: Implementation, as the teachers integrate this new method of working as a learning organization.

Stage 3: Institutionalization refers to the acquisition of new behaviors or attitudes. This stage is critical to ensure sustainment of the PLC if it is successfully integrated. During this period, teachers come to view the PLC as an invaluable and well-anchored practice that nurtures mutual growth, collegiality, and a shared decision-making system that promotes a shared vision and learning for every member. For the PLC to be successfully implemented and to evolve, the school-team must engage in open dialogue.

5.1.12—*Assist My School-Team in Finding and Applying the Most Effective Educational Practices for the Specific Needs of the Students*

Two fundamental principles guide the actions of the successful supervisor: the development of the teachers' professional skills and the use and production of data (Archambault & Dumais, 2012). Improving teaching ultimately improves student achievement.

The supervisor must promote new teaching strategies inside their school as well as educate their teachers on winning practices going on elsewhere. In this regard, it is important to note that funding from the professional development committee (prescribed in the employee collective agreement) should be allocated for certain priorities.

5.2—*KNOW HOW TO DO* IN HUMAN RELATIONS

In this section, we have retained 18 *know how to do* in human relations pertaining to transversal leadership skills (4), methodology (6), cooperation (1), communication (1), and ethics (6).

- Use *relational* leadership: Encourage communication, consultation, and discussion among the teachers.
- Use *transformational* leadership: Inspire, stimulate, optimize the potential of each teacher, and empower them toward self-reliance.
- Delegate support duties and responsibilities to the vice principal and to teachers and closely monitor.
- Maintain staff awareness of the main orientations and general objectives regarding student achievement.
- Objectively analyze the school's climate.
- Develop and implement a pluriannual supervision plan for my teachers.
- Use data collection and analysis tools.
- Agree to the mutual expectations during the individual/group supervision process.
- Guide each supervised teacher to self-evaluate and set professional growth objectives.
- Provide constructive individual/group feedback following supervision activities and follow up accordingly.
- Consult school district services for specific expertise.
- Communicate clearly with my teachers.
- Encourage and organize development activities based on the school's needs and those of the teachers.
- Use differentiated supervision for behaviors related to the motivation, commitment, and professional competence of the supervised teacher.
- Ensure that the rules of confidentiality are respected.
- Acknowledge the personal/collective contributions and successes of my teachers.
- Demonstrate managerial courage in certain supervision situations.
- Declare my intentions and explain my supervision actions.

Leadership

5.2.1—*Use Relational Leadership: Encourage Communication, Consultation, and Discussion Among the Teachers*

The relational skills of the supervisor are preambles to any successful supervision practice. According to Boutet and Rousseau (2002), regardless of their position on the ladder, the supervisor must have good relational skills. In other words, they must be able to establish effective interpersonal communication with the persons they supervise, but also with the other members of the organization to avoid creating any conflict with the different intervention stakeholders.

Therefore, to be effective, supervisors must analyze their relationship with the persons they supervise to be better able to sustain it. Weisinger (2013) put forth that, to analyze a relationship, the supervisor must examine the different viewpoints to be able to better plan future actions, whether the context is a single meeting or a more long-term relationship. The supervisor must essentially be able to consider their teachers' feelings, moods, and needs, and evaluate accordingly.

In short, these relational leadership capabilities can be aligned with skills associated with emotional intelligence. Bradberry and Greaves (2009) found that managing relationships (one aspect of social competence) also involved the three other skills associated with emotional intelligence, namely, self-esteem, self-confidence, and social awareness; it is the aptitude to use our awareness of our emotions and that of others to efficiently manage the interactions we have with them. This ability enhances communication (Bradberry & Greaves, 2009).

5.2.2—Use Transformational Leadership: Inspire, Stimulate, Optimize the Potential of Each Teacher, and Empower Them Toward Self-Reliance

Principals who are supervisors play a significant role in the empowerment of their teachers, who in turn also become leaders. These supervisors thus become builders of individual and organizational skills (Glanz & Zepeda, 2015).

The supervisor who employs effective transformational leadership guides their teachers to look beyond their personal interests and embrace those of their group or organization. For Tremblay and Simard (2005), this pedagogical leader represents a source of inspiration, a model that their teachers can emulate. This successful "coach" thus identifies the strengths and weaknesses of their staff and encourages them to develop intellectually.

Based on Burns (1978) and elements of charismatic leadership, Bass (1985) drew a portrait of transformational leadership. This type of leadership encourages teachers to (1) broaden their horizons, deepen their understanding of the group's objectives and mission, and own them, and (2) look beyond their personal interests to consider the bigger picture.

Transformational leadership houses four dimensions: charisma, inspiration, intellectual stimulation, and individual recognition.

1. Using *charisma*, the leader rallies the members around a vision and instills pride, respect, trust, and the conviction of accomplishing something important.
2. Using *inspiration*, the leader injects courage, uses symbols to reinforce and center the team's efforts, and clearly explains important objectives.
3. Using *stimulation*, the leader attracts intelligence, rationality, and rigorousness in the solving of problems.
4. Using individual *recognition*, the leader pays attention to each person and views each one as being unique.

5.2.3—Delegate Support Duties and Responsibilities to the Vice Principal and to Teachers and Closely Monitor

Over the last few decades, the shared leadership approach has gained in popularity with educators, researchers, and decision makers alike (Hallinger & Heck, 2010;

Klar, Huggins, & Roessler, 2016; Louis et al., 2010). This growing interest may be explained by the fact that education stakeholders generally recognize that indeed, supervisors are not superhuman; they do not know and cannot do everything. The supervisor must admit their limits and set priorities for themselves and delegate responsibilities to their vice principals or to a teacher or group of teachers. This depends on the ability the supervisor has to delegate, to trust, and to ask for updates on each process.

According to Vachon, Guertin, and Jutras (2013), the principal and the education consultant who join forces to establish realistic and effective measures for an array of situational contexts benefit from this interaction by creating a work alliance, strategizing their interventions accordingly, mobilizing resources, sharing their practices, and finding ways to self-regulate. This dyad may also be between the principal and vice principal or be expanded using the expertise of the education consultant or that of another teacher in the school.

5.2.4—Maintain Staff Awareness of the Main Orientations and General Objectives Regarding Student Achievement

Successful supervisors are those who insist that their school's orientation inspire teachers in their practice as well as in their professional development (Brassard et al., 2004). This inspiring orientation is referred to as *mobilization*. Strong mobilization can be described as a series of behaviors that a specific group of individuals decides to voluntarily adopt in a discretionary manner (Tremblay & Simard, 2005). The group leader expresses a clear direction to their team and mobilizes them toward a common vision (Bourbeau, 2010). Mobilizing also means calling to action, be it one person or a group; it is strength in numbers. While this call to action articulates targeted objectives, the members have the latitude to decide which way they want to go. This approach therefore enables the members to innovate, experiment, and take calculated risks (Bourbeau, 2010).

These behaviors also translate to a form of forward action that goes beyond prescribed duties (Tremblay & Simard, 2005). Indeed, mobilization supposes that the persons involved already possess a certain level of motivation toward the object of the mobilization. For example, a teacher is mobilized when they voluntarily deploy above-normal efforts to produce work or teamwork of quality and added value.

Finally, for mobilization to occur in an organization, the supervisor must satisfy these four conditions: clarity, competence, influence, and recognition.

Method

5.2.5—Objectively Analyze the School's Climate

The *organizational climate*, according to Schermerhorn, Hunt, Osborn, and de Billy (2014), is the perception employees have of their workplace and particularly the ambiance, the relationships with colleagues, and the ongoing supervision.

The *school climate* pertains to the atmosphere surrounding social relations, the value given to individuals, the school's educational mission, and the institution as a living environment. Janosz, Georges, and Parent (1998) identified several facets to school climate: relational, educational, security, justice, and belonging. A school's general climate is characterized by five main dimensions: confidence, openness, self-fulfillment, interdependence, and personal or organizational effectiveness (Tardif, 2005).

The issue of school climate has been examined by several authors. Sangsue and Vorpe (2004) studied the psychosocial climate in schools through the perceptions and feelings of individuals toward how their school functions. These authors found that school climate had a significant impact on stress level, work satisfaction, perception of violence, and the physical well-being of both teachers and students. A good school climate was indeed shown to predict a high level of satisfaction in teachers and students regarding their school as well as a perception of less violence within the school, which confirms that the quality of the atmosphere in a school may be as important for teachers as it is for students (Sangsue & Vorpe, 2004).

In successful teacher supervision, the supervisor always establishes a climate of respect and trust with the supervised teacher to nurture mutual cooperation (Bouchamma & Basque, 2012). Although built over time, this relationship does remain fragile, as it takes place within a context of authority (Paquay, 2007).

The supervisor preserves the relationship of trust with their teachers by knowing how to maintain balance between assistance and pedagogical control (Lapointe, Brassard, Garon, Girard, & Ramdé, 2011). Sustaining a nonhierarchical relationship also facilitates the supervision process (Bouchamma, 2007).

To create an environment that supports learning, efforts must be made to close the gaps between the teachers' perceptions, needs, and aspirations regarding the environment. Negative attitudes have a negative impact and ultimately influence their performance. In this perspective, professional development can help change these perceptions.

Ultimately, what the students think is just as important as what their teachers think because they are also stakeholders in the education system.

Wang and Degol (2016) identified four domains relative to school climate, namely, security, community, achievement, and institutional environment (see Table 5.1).

5.2.6—Develop and Implement a Pluriannual Supervision Plan for My Teachers

It is crucial that supervisors know the needs of their teachers and students to provide the best possible interventions (Leurebourg, 2013). The supervisor must therefore ensure that a proper pedagogical supervision plan is developed and established in the school (Brassard et al., 2004). This plan must take into account several complementary factors, such as the existing laws and programs, students' outcomes, and the school district's analyses and recommendations (Savoie-Zajc, 2008).

We are reminded that formal supervision consists of an initial interview, one or more in-class observations, feedback after each observation visit, and one or more meetings to exchange or evaluate the situation once the process has been completed.

The duration of the supervision plan may vary depending on numerous factors, such as the number of supervised persons in the school, the presence or absence of a vice principal, the number and importance of the school's priorities, and whether other schools are involved.

Table 5.1. Conceptualization and Categorization of School Climate (based on Wang & Degol, 2016)

Security	Social and emotional	Respect, absence of intimidation and harassment.
	Discipline	Conflict resolution, clarity, fairness, consistency, compliance to the school's rules.
	Physical	Reduced violence and aggressions, the students feel safe, presence of supervisors and surveillance measures.
Community	Roles	Involvement of community members and parents' participation.
	Relationships	Trust, affiliations between the students and the school-team.
	Solidarity	Sense of belonging to the school, extracurricular activities.
	Respect for diversity	Fairness, autonomy, decision-making opportunities
Academic achievement	Principal	The supervisor and the other staff members support the teachers and have open communication.
	Teaching and learning	Instructional quality, student evaluation, teacher involvement in the educational activities, student motivation, teachers' high expectations, established learning objectives.
	Professional development	Examination of teaching practices, professional growth opportunities.
Institutional environment	Physical	Design/decor, cleanliness, maintenance, construction quality.
	Structural organization	Size of the school's classrooms, group training, schedules.
	Availability of resources	Presence of relevant didactic material, shared resources.

5.2.7—Use Data Collection and Analysis Tools

Data Collection Using Tools

A good supervisor collects data using structured observation grids to organize the gathered data to better formulate clear and objective decisions (Boutet & Rousseau, 2002).

If the observation is not structured (i.e., is not done using grid items to measure the phenomenon in question), the supervisor can easily fall prey to subjectivity. Using these grids is crucial, whether they are existing tools or adapted ones. They must be shared with the supervised teacher to enable each party to know which elements are to be measured (e.g., questioning, classroom management). Performing a structured observation using valid tools helps to objectively collect data and also avoid possible biases and errors. When these valid tools are used, the data collected will enable the supervisor to effectively:

- support and document their decisions regarding the supervised teacher to warrant professional development and improve teaching practices;
- upgrade practices and give recognition where it is due; and
- be more objective and thus alleviate any possible judgment errors.

Indeed, decisions based on data gathered using valid observation tools undoubtedly carry more weight.

Data Analysis

The supervisor's decisions are based on clear objectives previously agreed on by both parties and on an analysis of the data collected during the observations. At the end of the discussions with the supervised teacher, a decision is rendered based on observable and measureable facts and not on perceptions, rumors, or hearsay. With the help of the supervisor, the teacher determines which aspects they want to work on during the year to improve their practice. Both parties then come to an agreement regarding the objectives for professional growth and the measures to attain the objectives.

Finally, the supervisor must have the ability to analyze the data relative to a problem, and more importantly, to summarize these analyzed elements. Any decision must take into account several factors, such as the objectives of the supervision and the context in which the teacher evolves.

5.2.8—*Agree to the Mutual Expectations During the Individual/Group Supervision Process*

For these support actions to be successful and to facilitate progress, the supervisor and the supervised teacher must agree on which objective is to be the focus in their process.

The supervision process must center on the teacher's needs. The supervisor's role is basically one of trust, where they exchange ideas with the teacher and work with them to find solutions to improve both teaching and learning (Gall & Acheson, 2011).

If we are in a system without supervision programs, it is possible to refer to the list of teacher skills to identify the aspects most likely to be the object of supervision (Danielson, 2014).

The objectives must be *SMART*, and data collection must be based on grids that are shared between the supervisor and the supervised teacher to avoid possible errors, such as observing something unrelated to the desired objective.

When ambiguity reigns, supervision may be a source of concern that generates stress. Both partners must be on the same page in terms of the purpose of the process and the established objectives. They each have the same data collection grids. In other words, the supervisor is responsible for ensuring that the rules of the game are clear and that the teacher is responsible for their professional development. Indeed, Paquay (2007) concurred that the worst thing is vagueness. If the facets of the object of supervision are not clearly defined, if the reference criteria are not detailed, this may arbitrarily sway in favor of the person who has the most power and who will essentially have the last word. Having clear objectives is therefore key. The criteria for quality must also be considered, and how they relate to teaching practice/competence standards. Therein lie the symbols of formative dialogue (Paquay, 2007).

To avoid confusion and related stress, it is in the best interest of the supervisor to dissipate any ambiguity surrounding their role, as in situations where the supervised teacher becomes unsure of the supervisor's expectations of them. The role of each party in the process must be clearly outlined, and both parties must remain open-minded to give and receive in the spirit of mutual collaboration (Fortin & Pharand, 2005).

5.2.9 — Guide Each Supervised Teacher to Self-Evaluate and Set Professional Growth Objectives

To effectively guide their teachers to reflect on their practice and to self-evaluate, the supervisor must first be able to perform their own self-assessment. This leader is, in fact, a reflective companion, a thinker who helps someone else think. Indeed, Boutet and Pharand (2008) viewed this reflective facilitator as a practitioner capable of exteriorizing, of explaining, and of formalizing their *know how to act* in regards to proven theories, while at the same time enabling the other to also think themselves, about themselves.

Helping the supervised teacher self-evaluate their practices is teaching them to build their professional identity. In this perspective, teacher self-evaluation does not only pertain to measured performance; the teacher actually creates this *professionality* through the cognitive evaluation of their pedagogical effectiveness. This process of self-evaluation and reinforcement of the sense of efficacy is indeed fundamental to the production of teaching practices (Safourcade & Alava, 2009).

The effective supervisor is also capable of asking the right questions to stimulate their teachers to reflect and to determine personal professional development goals. Burns and Badiali (2015) referred to this action as the supervisor's "reflection routine" and proposed that these leaders prepare a series of questions with their supervised staff. This routine makes it possible to engage in meaningful reflective conversation, which in turn enhances the understanding and analysis of practices. In other words, asking the other significant questions helps them clarify their thoughts and feelings (Weisinger, 2013).

Ultimately, the supervisor's job is to encourage the teacher to engage in a continuous process of introspection that leads them to self-evaluate (Nolan & Hoover, 2008). Among the proposed measures are teaching the teacher to create a professional portfolio, or how to use one; this encourages reflection, which in turn helps improve their practice. Using the portfolio as a self-supervision tool thus contributes to demonstrating their skills, abilities, and creativity, and supports reflection and professional growth (Desjardins, 2002). While portfolios can also serve to collect relevant data over a long period of time (Tucker et al., 2003), they must not constitute their only source of information. Furthermore, the supervisor must provide clear directives to their teachers and give them enough time and guidance to develop and use their portfolio (Attinello, Lare, & Waters, 2006).

5.2.10 — *Provide Constructive Individual/Group Feedback Following Supervision Activities and Follow Up Accordingly*

A good pedagogical supervisor always provides their supervised teacher with significant feedback and discusses their observations relative to the preestablished objectives, in the spirit of improvement (Boutet & Rousseau, 2002). To do so, the supervisor must know how to formulate their positive criticism. According to Bradberry and Greaves (2009), proper critiquing contains the expression of an opinion and the presentation of a viable solution.

Giving feedback requires prudence, as it may place the supervisor in a vulnerable position. Weisinger (2013) found that because of this vulnerability, people are often on the defensive when they receive a critique, which is why the person giving the feedback often feels unsettled. This author uses the *hard pill to swallow* metaphor to illustrate critiquing: it is usually difficult and disagreeable to take, but ultimately necessary. When the person receives the feedback, they may become more aware of the way they are being perceived, change behaviors that may appear inadequate, and consequently grow in the experience. In other words, when critiquing someone, you are helping them do the same (Weisinger, 2013).

Cooperation

5.2.11 — *Consult School District Services for Specific Expertise*

Studies highlight the importance for supervisors to cooperate with other education stakeholders to pool their combined talents. According to Arpin and Capra (2008), one invaluable skill in the professional arsenal of the supervisor is to be able to collaborate with other actors within the system. It is increasingly necessary to both encourage and combine the diverse talents of these stakeholders to better respond to the educational needs of all concerned (Arpin & Capra, 2008).

School boards exist to provide services to meet the needs of school principals, not the other way around. School leaders and their teachers should be able to count on these services with highly qualified individuals who possess the necessary expertise to address specific and sometimes difficult issues and to provide professional development opportunities for school employees.

Communication

5.2.12 — *Communicate Clearly With My Teachers*

Communication is the process of emission and reception of meaningful messages (Schermerhorn, Hunt, Osborn, & de Billy, 2014) but also the transmission and most importantly the understanding of a message between two individuals (McShane & Benabou, 2008).

Effective communication between a supervisor and their teachers has been shown to enhance school organization and climate (Halawah, 2005), interpersonal skills, and work satisfaction (De Nobile & McCormick, 2008).

In the ever-evolving context of school management and because of the pedagogical dimension of the supervisor's role, information, collaboration, and communication are increasingly meaningful in the relationships they have with their teachers. Here, this communication is often an indirect or complementary component of other concepts studied by researchers, such as school climate (Halawah, 2005; MacNeil, Prater, & Busch, 2009).

A good supervisor is an active listener who understands the actual needs of the supervised teacher. According to Melchers (2005), supervisor efficacy is often defined by the ability to communicate, regardless of who it is and whether it is a one-on-one or group situation. Whether it's communicating their vision, bringing a teacher to order, or introducing reform, each communication must be clear and effective (Melchers, 2005).

MITRA Consultants en services aux entreprises proposes five levels of active listening. A person who listens with empathy is totally in the moment. They notice the other person's behaviors and are able to recognize certain signs of hesitance, doubt, or approbation. A good listener incites the speaker to listen with the same intensity.

- First, listen with intent.
  - Ask yourself "What is the goal of my listening?"
  - Examples:
    - My goal, for now, is to discover the real reason for this teacher's lack of satisfaction.
    - My goal is to gather as much information as possible to enable me to evaluate a quality problem in my teacher's work.
    - My unique goal is to listen attentively so that I can show them that they are wrong when it is my turn to speak (pay attention to knowing your limitations as a listener).
    - Give yourself the necessary space and time.
- Listen to understand rather than to evaluate.
  - Understand the other person's point of view and try not to change their point of view or the person themselves.
  - Accept to listen to a different point of view.
  - Accept that you must first understand before being understood.
- Be aware of the behaviors, words, and phrases that distract you and make you defensive.
  - Examples:
    - We should never work like that!
    - Am I prejudiced toward this person?
- A good listener listens with their mind, their body, and their heart.
  - What do you see, hear, smell (nonverbal)?
    - Emotions you notice.
    - Unspoken demands.
  - What does this person want: commitment, actions, guarantees, security?
    - What positive results are they expecting?
    - Do *not* do two things at once. Give 100% of your attention.

To deliver your message, it is important to choose the best method of communication to fit the context. Depending on the nature and content of the messages to be delivered, the method used (verbal or written) will transfer the information more effectively (McShane & Benabou, 2008).

Moreover, regardless of their position on the ladder, the pedagogical supervisor must possess good relational skills to be able to establish effective interpersonal communication not only with the persons they supervise but also with the other members of the organization so as to avoid conflicts with the other intervention stakeholders (Boutet & Rousseau, 2002).

It must be said that the supervisor must also pay attention to the nonverbal aspects of their communication because activity or nonactivity, words or silence, everything holds a message (Fortin & Pharand, 2005).

Ethics

5.2.13—*Encourage and Organize Development Activities Based on the School's Needs and Those of the Teachers*

Every supervision process must lead to professional development. The supervisor and the supervised teachers must both develop an annual professional growth plan that reflects the priorities of the school and the needs expressed.

We are reminded that the democratic principle of professional development is that every supervised teacher is invited to make their professional development needs known and express their views on how these needs can be addressed (Gordon, 2015). This author argued that the members of the school-team should be involved in the decisions pertaining to the development of the school's professional training program.

As regards the teachers' needs, the supervisor could ask the teachers' professional development committee to determine these needs for the entire staff, or by department, cycle, or even level. This would be an excellent way to involve the teachers and mobilize them. These data can then be used in elaborating the professional development program for the teachers.

5.2.14—*Use Differentiated Supervision for Behaviors Related to the Motivation, Commitment, and Professional Competence of the Supervised Teacher*

Because teachers are not all at the same level personally and professionally, their needs regarding supervision may differ. In other words, supervision must be adapted to each person (Bouchamma & Michaud, 2014). The supervisor must be aware of the level of professional and personal maturity of the supervised teacher to be able to situate their supervision interviews and develop a plan that fits their needs.

As Dupuis (2004) explained, the education system is a field where individual needs may vary depending on the level of experience of the teacher. For example, young adults just starting in the teaching profession feel the existential need to assert themselves professionally while searching for models, masters, and mentors to help them reach their goals, whereas teachers in the middle of their career feel the need to help the younger teachers to satisfy their generativity. An enlightened approach can therefore align the basic needs of both groups, for everyone's benefit (Dupuis, 2004).

Professional development must therefore take into account the personal and professional characteristics of the teacher. Girard, McLean, and Morissette (1992) identified a typology composed of two groups of behaviors, namely, behaviors related to motivation and commitment and behaviors associated with professional competence.

Behavioral Indicators of Motivation and Commitment

- the willingness to take on responsibilities
- the desire for accomplishment in a particular task
- the willingness to participate in a project (from inaction to action)
- tenacity
- the willingness to take the initiative (search for new approaches)
- the willingness to make decisions (self-reliance in the tasks undertaken)
- the desire to be flexible (adapt to change)

Behavioral Indicators of Professional Competence

- the participation in teaching and pedagogical supervision activities
- an understanding of the job requirements
- the ability to respect deadlines
- the ability to solve problems
- the use of appropriate teaching methods
- the ability to take on responsibilities (to establish standards, take risks, demonstrate efficacy, and self-motivate)

Ultimately, good supervision is anchored in the context. The school leader must hone their ability to analyze a given context and apply supervision principles that correspond to the situation. A single supervision model can therefore not be used in every school and every situation. On the other hand, individual supervision supported by the appropriate data is likely to lead to constructive changes (Gordon, 2016).

In this perspective, Nolan and Hoover (2004), in their study on peer coaching, positioned the exploration of supervision (and evaluation) practices in relation to teacher characteristics and their professional growth.

5.2.15—Ensure That the Rules of Confidentiality Are Respected

During a supervision interview, the supervised teacher may express their desire that certain aspects of the conversation remain confidential. Depending on the context, it would be wise at the end of the interview to determine which segments are targeted in this confidentiality agreement. In the case of an interview leading to disciplinary measures, the supervisor cannot uphold confidentiality. In other words, the best attitude to adopt (for both parties involved) is *discretion*. According to Ducommun (2008), the rules of confidentiality ensure a neutral, nonjudgmental space that supports the supervised person by guiding them inward to reflect and to self-evaluate.

5.2.16—Acknowledge the Personal/Collective Contributions and Successes of My Teachers

The effective supervisor shows their appreciation and recognizes the accomplishments of their supervised teachers. Maxwell (2003) wrote that when school leaders transfer their authority to people to whom they wish to delegate power, they must convey their belief in the other's abilities. This empowers them into believing that they will indeed succeed, and in turn this enables other people around them to feel supported and guided by this authority.

Weisinger (2013) wrote that showing appreciation and recognition in the workplace takes place through a supportive relationship in which the supervisor has secured the commitment of the teacher to take action to reach a goal, and thus provides them with the encouragement they need to pursue this goal. In fact, this appreciation and recognition directs the other to act (Weisinger, 2013).

When someone is encouraged during a specific action, they are inclined to repeat this action to win praise or reinforcement once more. In other words, encouragement incites a person to repeat the behavior in the hopes of receiving other approbation (Weisinger, 2013). Ultimately, the notion of empowerment is omnipresent when expressing recognition in the workplace, in whatever form that may be.

5.2.17—Demonstrate Managerial Courage in Certain Supervision Situations

In individual supervision, the collected and analyzed data may oblige the supervisor to request that the teacher concerned deal with a particular problem situation, to change one or more behaviors, or to improve one or more skills. When these situations arise, appropriate support must be provided. It is certainly not the most interesting part of this leader's duties, but it must be done. Regardless of the amount of experience the supervisor may have, it takes managerial courage, and in certain cases, this leader may need to consult with human resources.

5.2.18—Declare My Intentions and Explain My Supervision Actions

According to Weisinger (2013), it is critical that supervised individuals understand the reason why one choice is preferred over another. Weisinger (2013) also argued that in the context of emotional intelligence, explaining what you do is of great relevance, as the others become aware that you are conscious of how they may perceive your apparent actions (or lack thereof) and the consequences of a negative perception on them.

The supervised teacher must be aware of the objectives of their supervisor. Is their supervision centered on discussion, guidance, support, improving practices, solving a problem, or evaluating the teacher? It is critical that teachers have a good impression of the process and its advantages. When declaring your intentions, wrote Weisinger (2013), you are basically telling the other person what you want. When you have clarified what you want (and of course considering what the other person wants), it is easier to adopt the strategy that will get you where you want to go.

The goals of the supervision must thus always be clearly expressed to the supervised teacher to avoid any interpretation that could hinder the process.

For an overview of the main *know how to do* of an effective supervisor, see Table 5.2.

Table 5.2. Synthesis of the Main *Know How to Do* of the Effective Supervisor

	Pedagogical Know How to Do	Know How to Do *in Human Relations*
Leadership	5.1.1 Use pedagogical leadership: Promote my vision of the school system, my educational orientations and values; encourage the professional development of my staff; support pedagogical projects and innovations. 5.1.2 Use situational leadership: Focus on the students' needs and the school's education priorities. 5.1.3 Manage ethnocultural diversity in my school.	5.2.1 Use relational leadership: Encourage communication, consultation, and discussion among the teachers. 5.2.2 Use transformational leadership: Inspire, stimulate, optimize the potential of each teacher, and empower them toward self-reliance 5.2.3 Delegate support duties and responsibilities to the vice principal and to teachers and closely monitor. 5.2.4 Maintain staff awareness of the main orientations and general objectives regarding student achievement.
Method	5.1.4 Organize my time to make teacher supervision a priority. 5.1.5 Supervise the attainment of the achievement objectives. 5.1.6 Encourage and support the pedagogical projects of my teachers and assist them in their professional development related to the school's priorities and the students' needs. 5.1.7 Supervise the compliance to national/local policies and those of the school in matters of pedagogy. 5.1.8 Financially support my teachers' pedagogical projects and professional development needs. 5.1.9 Structure organization to enable teachers to attend professional development activities. 5.1.10 Perform teacher supervision with no subjectivity.	5.2.5 Objectively analyze the school's climate. 5.2.6 Develop and implement a pluriannual supervision plan for my teachers. 5.2.7 Use data collection and analysis tools. 5.2.8 Agree to the mutual expectations during the individual/group supervision process. 5.2.9 Guide each supervised teacher to self-evaluate and set professional growth objectives. 5.2.10 Provide constructive individual/group feedback following supervision activities and follow up accordingly.
Cooperation	5.1.11 Establish work groups/PLCs in my school and encourage peer collaboration. 5.1.12 Assist my school-team in finding and applying the most effective educational practices for the specific needs of the students.	5.2.11 Consult school district services for specific expertise.
Communication		5.2.12 Communicate clearly with my teachers.
Ethics		5.2.13 Encourage and organize development activities based on the school's needs and those of the teachers. 5.2.14 Use differentiated supervision for behaviors related to the motivation, commitment, and professional competence of the supervised teacher. 5.2.15 Ensure that the rules of confidentiality are respected. 5.2.16 Acknowledge the personal/collective contributions and successes of my teachers. 5.2.17 Demonstrate managerial courage in certain supervision situations. 5.2.18 Declare my intentions and explain my supervision actions.

Can you think of any other pedagogical know how to do *or* know how to do *in human relations?*

Chapter Six

The *Know How to Be* Every Supervisor Should Possess

Supervision can be viewed as both a philosophy and a practice; thus the concepts of communal living, collegiality, openness to collaboration, and ethics have become imperatives (Garman & Holland, 2016). *Knowing how to be* enables the supervisor to use their personal resources (aptitudes, qualities, emotions, or physiological aspects) in a given situation or context (Le Boterf, 2002).

According to Rousseau (2005), a supervisor must be trustworthy, conscientious, and open-minded, in addition to using tact and being an excellent listener. These are but a few *know how to be* used by an effective supervisor, which we will explore in this chapter.

6.1—PEDAGOGICAL *KNOW HOW TO BE*

In this section, two *know how to be* are presented related to ethics:

- Be consistent in my educational values and my professional practice.
- Welcome pedagogical initiatives.

Ethics

6.1.1—Be Consistent in My Educational Values and My Professional Practice

Each day, the supervisor must define, repeat, illustrate, and most importantly include the school's educational values in their words and actions. In other words, the supervisor must continuously model these educational values.

6.1.2—Welcome Pedagogical Initiatives

The effective supervisor guides their teachers to reflect on the supervision process, which requires a transfer of complex pedagogical knowledge within reflective conversations on teaching and learning. Discussing student learning with teachers can, however, represent a challenge for many supervisors (Hazi & Rucinski, 2009). Research emphasizes the importance of encouraging teachers to develop pedagogical initiatives by providing financial support for projects aimed at innovation in both teaching and learning. The literature also supports the need to be open-minded toward teachers' initiatives.

According to Ponticell (2015), supervision that is creative helps teachers to be more independent in their practice, enables them to voluntarily share with their peers, and facilitates their growth and experimentation. This not only encourages teachers to be more authentic but also boosts their self-esteem and enhances their ability to self-evaluate. Indeed, creative supervision:

- encourages teachers to think for themselves in matters pertaining to objectives, curriculum, organization and content, methods of teaching, and methods of evaluation;
- encourages teachers to share their thoughts voluntarily with the supervisor and coworkers;
- never stifles the inclination of a teacher to experiment with his own ideas, though the dangers of experimentation are kept in mind;
- does more than encourage: it inspires teachers to be themselves and to do for themselves; it imbues them with self-confidence and the power of self-evaluation.

Finally, the principal must encourage discussion to identify the best solutions for each situation. Solutions resulting from peer consultations are more likely to be applied by teachers than those from the top down.

According to Mailhot (2010), principals must basically be able to develop a flexible attitude in a variety of different contexts. The first solution that comes to mind may not necessarily be the best one. Allowing the employee to express their point of view and also propose ideas for effective action is among several possible options. Moreover, using discussion to develop the most viable and practical solution for the organization, the one people will most likely adhere to, is far better than a unilateral decision without consultation.

In light of this, in an effort to favor the development of educational initiatives, couldn't a school or school district organize, for example, one day per year to present new projects or again to recognize the most original project of the year?

6.2—*KNOW HOW TO BE* IN HUMAN RELATIONS

In this section, nine *know how to be* in cross-curricular competencies are presented pertaining to method (1), cooperation (1), ethics (2), and emotional intelligence (5).

- Be flexible and available.
- Be sociable.
- Be fair.
- Believe in the progress and professional development of each supervised person.
- Possess a strong sense of personal efficacy.

- Manage my stress and emotions.
- Consider the emotional and affective dimension of the supervised person and show empathy.
- Be a good listener.
- Make people comfortable and trusting.

Method

6.2.1—Be Flexible and Available

School leaders perform their duties in an environment that is constantly evolving due to decreased resources, teachers' expectations, parental demands, and new reforms and regulations, among others. Consequently, they must be on their toes and continuously adjust their objectives and strategic choices (Bélair, Lebel, Sorin, Roy, & Lafortune, 2010). Flexibility is thus evidenced in the supervisor's ability to successfully adapt their management style depending on the situation.

Following their meta-analysis, Marzano, Waters, and McNulty (2016) proposed a list of specific behaviors associated with this *know how to be*:

- adapt my leadership style depending on what the situation calls for;
- be directive or nondirective, depending on what the situation calls for;
- encourage people to express varied and opposing opinions; and
- be comfortable making important changes in how things are done.
- be flexible.

The supervisor must also be available: for example, an "open door" policy is a good practice, as it relays the notion that meeting with teachers is a priority. Furthermore, the effective supervisor lets their staff know when they are available for individual meetings.

The notion of flexibility in supervision is closely associated with the concept of democratic leadership in which the supervisor cultivates a climate favoring participation, the sharing of ideas, and such virtues as honesty, open-mindedness, and compassion.

Here, three principles of a strong democracy apply to supervision: (1) inclusion of stakeholders in pedagogical dialogue and decision making; (2) integration, as democracy is embedded in all aspects of classroom/school supervision; and (3) internalization, where democracy becomes a way of life, a habitual way of dealing with people and situations (Gordon & Boone, 2014).

Gordon (2016) also proposed seven principles related to supervision. They are: (1) grounded in democracy; (2) collective; (3) affirmative; (4) fostering authentic instruction; (5) reflective; (6) addressing cultural diversity; and (7) the importance of context. According to this author, what is good supervision for one particular school evolves as the school changes, and what is good supervision for one teacher changes as the teacher develops. In other words, because supervision remains contextual, supervisors must develop their flexibility in this regard.

Lastly, for practical reasons, the principal may increase their availability by making their personal calendar known to their school-team, thus making it easier for teachers to make an appointment at times when their supervisor is available to meet with them (Zepeda, Lanoue, Creel, & Price, 2015).

Cooperation

6.2.2—Be Sociable

Personality traits are lasting characteristics that determine a person's behavior. In the early 1990s, a five-factor personality model was developed that groups together the five main dimensions of personal characteristics.

These five dimensions, also known as the *Big Five*, are: extraversion, agreeableness, conscientiousness, emotional stability (neuroticism), and openness to experience. Sociability is part of the dimension of extraversion. Schermerhorn, Hunt, Osborn, and de Billy (2014) associated this dimension with the ability of a person to enter into relations with others. The extraverted person is communicative, sociable, and confident, while the introverted person is shy, reserved, and calm.

The supervisor must want to learn to know the persons they are supervising. According to Melchers (2005), to develop a trusting relationship with their teachers, supervisors must first learn to know them, understand their values, and show interest in them to better address their needs. Gordon (2008) put forth that this "knowledge of the other" is achieved through dialogue that enables both parties to reach a common ground, identify and discuss hypotheses, develop open-mindedness regarding change, mobilize the strengths of each party, integrate ideas, and envision effective solutions. In addition, dialogue can both inspire and enhance reflection. In a study led by Zepeda (2012), teachers who engaged in meaningful dialogue with their supervisors and other teachers were found to be more inclined to reflect on their practices and be more interested in the deeper issues of teaching and learning.

All things considered, compared to the hierarchical model, we much prefer the humanistic approach in teacher supervision, which has been and continues to be a winning method.

Ethics

6.2.3—Be Fair

Supervisors play a crucial role in ensuring the adoption of a mission and a vision of fairness in their school (Leithwood & Jantzi, 2000; Leithwood & Riehl, 2003).

The effective supervisor is fair and takes into account the interests of the supervised teacher and their professional growth. They also show a willingness to understand the teachers they supervise and to make available the necessary resources that support their development.

Supervisors must also be culturally receptive. They must define and promote a set of values and principles related to fairness and must demonstrate behaviors and attitudes that will enable them to consider each individual and group. To do so, successful supervisors learn to embrace diversity, conduct a self-evaluation, arbitrate differences, acquire and institutionalize cultural knowledge, and adapt to existing cultural contexts

Figure 6.1.   Equality versus Equity
Reference: www.symbioserh.ca

(Levin & Fullan, 2008). They seek to create and maintain positive ethical attitudes and motivating educational practices, encourage communication and transparency, and contribute resources toward cultural receptivity (Levin & Fullan, 2008).

Moreover, it is interesting to note that the concept of equality, which differs from fairness (equity), relates to the desire to offer the same thing for all. However, because supervisors do not all start at the same place, they have different needs, hence the need to differentiate supervision. This impartiality can thus be defined as an attitude with which we treat each person equitably as opposed to favoring our own interests (Prairat, 2013).

Ultimately, supervisors must be a model of social justice (Burns, Yendol-Hoppey, & Jacobs, 2015) for their supervised teachers, who will in turn use this *know how to be* with their students. This mission and vision of fairness is thus practiced and nurtured within the school. Establishing social justice, however, takes time and requires focus and commitment.

6.2.4 — Believe in the Progress and Professional Development of Each Supervised Person

Through their attitude and support, the supervisor must acknowledge and allow their supervised teacher to demonstrate their ability to succeed. They must construct their own ideas as to the teacher's profile and not be influenced by their own perceptions or what they may have learned about the person.

The effective supervisor firmly believes in their ability to help, support, and improve the teachers they are supervising. They are also open-minded, provide encouragement for the supervised teacher in their professional growth, and adjust their interventions accordingly.

To provide the right support for their supervised teacher, the supervisor must believe in the latter's potential for growth; everyone can learn, and no one fails (Prairat, 2013). Teachers need to hear from their supervisor that they believe in them and want them to succeed. Once they recognize and understand that their supervisor sincerely wants them to achieve their goals and that they are committed to helping them do so, teachers will start believing that they are capable of accomplishing the tasks that their supervisor has given them (Maxwell, 2003). Indeed, trusting the supervised person is another fundamental principle of teacher supervision.

Emotional Intelligence

6.2.5 — Possess a Strong Sense of Personal Efficacy

Before examining the sense of personal efficacy, it is relevant to mention Maslow's (1943) hierarchy of needs. This taxonomy, presented in the form of a pyramid, targets five needs that evolve into others once they are satisfied. The five needs are: physiological, security, social integration, self-esteem, and actualization. The need for self-esteem, which is of interest here, may be described as the need to feel proud and feel pride from others. To this is added the need for power, success, adequate performance, competence, and autonomy, among others. Satisfying these needs enhances self-esteem (Legendre, 2005).

Regarding the concept of self-efficacy or sense of personal efficacy, this is a significant theoretical contribution from Bandura (2003). This concept refers to the perceptions and beliefs of an individual regarding their abilities, resources, and capacity to complete a given task. The person's expectations regarding their personal efficacy determine the activities they choose, the efforts they are willing to deploy, and the level of perseverance invested in the process. People who believe strongly in their personal efficacy view difficult tasks as a challenge rather than as an obstacle to avoid, which increases their motivation. The belief that personal actions determine outcomes increases the sense of efficacy and of power, whereas the belief that results occur independently of what a person does creates apathy (Bandura, 2003).

The effective supervisor exudes confidence, which reassures the teachers under their supervision. Indeed, according to Fullan (2014), teachers expect that their leaders will help them find their way and maintain a sense of hope, regardless of the situation. Furthermore, the supervisor thus influences the teachers' behaviors by being perceived as the most capable person to address any challenges thrown their way. The supervisor is judged on their ability to direct their teachers toward resources that will most likely provide support.

As for the sense of competency, this can be built/consolidated several ways:

- positive experiences—they consolidate the feeling of self-esteem;
- vicarious learning—confidence is gained by observing others who have more experience;

- verbal persuasion—self-esteem is enhanced through the encouragement of a person who tells us that we are perfectly capable of succeeding in a task. When our peers, superiors, or supervisors congratulate our efforts and associate them with success, we become more motivated.

6.2.6—Manage My Stress and Emotions

Four groups of factors have an influence on the level of stress experienced in the workplace, namely, professional, individual, and socioeconomic factors and those related to personal life. Stress factors associated with professional life include the amount of qualitative and quantitative work (under/overworked), the lack of participation in decisions, the lack of information, ambiguity with regard to the role, conflict in the role, an ethical dilemma, the rate of professional growth, and physically demanding conditions (Schermerhorn, Hunt, Osborn, & de Billy, 2014, p. 599).

In the context of school management, the pedagogical role of supervisors, since the introduction of the accountability movement, carries much more weight. Does this signify that supervisors have an increasing amount of responsibilities? Lest we forget, an increased workload is among the professional factors associated with stress.

A supervisor may be more stressed when meeting with a difficult teacher, particularly if it involves applying disciplinary measures. The same situation occurs when the supervisor meets with the members of a PLC or a work group and must reprimand teachers who are resistant or uncooperative. Because principals encounter a multitude of stress-provoking situations during their supervision, managing their emotions is key.

Research on the subject of stress confirms that supervisors, in particular, deal with several stressful situations every day. Poirel (2009) explained that supervising can sometimes be compared to renouncing, to accepting to differ, delay, or even sacrifice administrative tasks so as to privilege quality human relations, by serving as an intermediary in managing conflicts and by accepting to attend numerous and lengthy meetings.

Another point regards the issues surrounding self-esteem and the emotions experienced, yet restrained. The supervisor usually does not show their anger to avoid confrontation and maintain a harmonious workplace, and they mask their anxiety to maintain their credibility and the "leader" image that is required of their position. Moreover, supervisors (principals) constantly compromise and are often left to deal with problems alone (Poirel, 2009).

6.2.7—Consider the Emotional and Affective Dimension of the Supervised Person and Show Empathy

We must first the position on the sympathy/empathy scale for supportive relationships, a tool that facilitates the learning of active listening and empathy.

Barbès (2001) used a barrel metaphor to illustrate the two types of aid. Viewed from above, it traces an axis of sympathy/empathy into three distinct zones (see Figure 6.2 and Table 6.1).

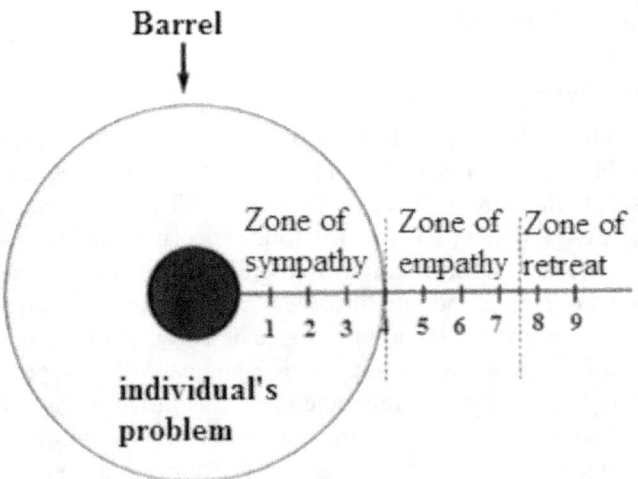

Figure 6.2. The Barrel Metaphor
Barbès, 2001

Table 6.1. A Comparison of Sympathy and Empathy (adapted from Barbès, 2001)

	Mechanism	Consequences	
	On the Supervisor	On the Teacher	On the Supervisor
Sympathy	Identify the teacher's problem Reply instead of the teacher Provide support, a problem-solving action for the other Victim/rescuer model (and eventually persecutor)	Feels they are being taken care of Is deresponsibilized Feels like they are being supported by a friend Thinks that their problem is solved	Feels closer to the teacher Confuses their needs with those of the teacher Tends to perceive the teacher as a friend Feels important Feels a bit overwhelmed Feels helpless Blames the supervised teacher
Empathy	Disidentification of the problem Leave the problem in the hands of the teacher Accountability approach Adult/adult model	Is invited to take charge of themselves Is held accountable Referred toward introspection, to look into their soul Feels profoundly understood, especially by themselves	Is truly close to the teacher Separates their needs with those of the teacher Is capable of confrontation when necessary May exercise an authoritative role

In Melchers (2005), the empathic leader is described as someone who is sensitive to the people around them and the signals they give out. They know how to put themselves in the other person's shoes and feel what the others are feeling, whether it be a person or a group. The leader who has empathy listens attentively and is capable of sharing the perspective of the person speaking to them.

In the realm of teacher supervision, the supervisor must master not only the inherent principles of the process but also the relational phenomena that go with it. During the process of supervision, the teacher may experience certain difficulties. The effective supervisor understands these difficulties, avoids putting the teacher down or making them feel guilty, and helps them solve their problem (Boutet and Rousseau, 2002).

According to Zepeda (2006), the ability to show empathy is one of the fundamental qualities of a successful supervisor. Indeed, when a supervisor demonstrates an empathic and authentic attitude, their practice is enriched with collaboration and cooperation. The supervisor must demonstrate a caring attitude to develop a trusting relationship with their team, which involves being a good listener to the different needs expressed. As highlighted by this author, beginning with their projects and ideas is always a winning strategy.

In conclusion, to help develop empathy with the teacher, Tremblay (1999) proposed the following protective techniques for support-giving situations: (1) learn to understand and set limits; (2) respect your vulnerability zones; (3) establish rules of conduct and respect them; and (4) use teamwork.

6.2.8—Be a Good Listener

The ability to listen not only is considered to be a necessary advantage in functions requiring communication (Schermerhorn, Hunt, Osborn, & de Billy, 2014) but can also be a proactive tool to help others to better understand a difficult situation, envision solutions in a more positive manner, and feel appreciated because of the support they receive (Weisinger, 2013).

In the context of accountability, supervisors must increasingly use shared leadership to improve teaching and learning. They must no longer limit themselves to conventional supervision but must rather evolve toward more innovative structures (such as professional learning communities [PLCs]) by engaging their teachers in pedagogical dialogue (Glickman, Gordon, & Ross-Gordon, 2014). Dialogue between supervisor and supervised teacher is ultimately beneficial to both parties, the result being a greater capacity to reflect on their respective practices and to exchange on issues related to the profession and to learning (Zepeda, 2012). It also establishes a common ground that nurtures discussion and creates a bridge to welcome change. In this perspective, the successful supervisor will seek to maximize the forces of each participant, integrate ideas, and provide opportunities for sustainable solutions (Gordon, 2008).

Finally, the supervisor must pay attention to their verbal and nonverbal language, as a shift may sometimes emerge between their words and what their actions and body language reveal. When there is too much deviation, the message may be contradictory (Schermerhorn, Hunt, Osborn, & de Billy, 2014).

6.2.9—Make People Comfortable and Trusting

Trust is necessary on every level (between superintendents and principals, between principals and their supervised teachers); each action must be trust-based (Zepeda, 2016). For this purpose, discussions and feedback are of the utmost importance. They must be reliable and positive. Conversation is even considered to be a determining factor in the relationship. As Scott (2004) put it, the conversation *is* the relationship.

Therefore, in the context of supervision, the relationship between supervisor and teacher must be one of trust. This relationship is built over time during formal or informal meetings. Gordon (2016) suggested, however, that trust extends beyond the principal-teacher relationship to encompass the processes, relations between people, and relations within the environment.

Because supervision involves a hierarchical relationship, the latter must be healthy so as to nurture trust, which is at the heart of any successful supervision practice. According to Paquay (2007), clearly communicating the rules is not enough; the supervised person must trust their supervisor. This trust is a work in progress and is tested every day, and because of the relation of power between employer and employee, it continues to remain fragile.

Arpin and Capra (2008) wrote that the effective supervisor creates a space without judgment. Welcoming the teachers, paying attention to them, giving them space and encouragement to enable them to share their successes and questions, discovering what interests them, embracing their talents—all this creates a positive climate that fosters learning. The time spent listening and sharing encourages pedagogical actions, the creation of productive relationships, and the establishment of a trusting environment where it is professionally allowed to say everything without being judged by peers and where mistakes are rather opportunities for growth.

That said, we reiterate that the most strategic supervision calls on the strengths of peers. Indeed, school principals who succeed are those who lead from within the school rather than from the top down, through a reinforcement of trust, a collaborative sharing of information and ideas, and symmetrical dialogue (Gordon, 2016). For example, mentoring or sponsorship by an experienced peer has been shown to have a positive influence on the self-esteem of young teachers (Rhodes & Beneicke, 2002).

Finally, for a supervisor to be successful, trust is the key. Everything they do depends on the trust teachers have in their ability to ensure sound school management and supervision that works (Zepeda, Lanoue, Creel, & Price, 2015). Trust can be worn down, however, when decisions fail to focus on student achievement, which is the ultimate goal of productive supervision.

For an overview of the main *know how to be* of an effective supervisor, see Table 6.2.

Table 6.2. Synthesis of the Main *Know How to Be* of an Effective Supervisor

	Pedagogical Know How to Be	Know How to Be *in Human Relations*
Method		6.2.1 Be flexible and available.
Cooperation		6.2.2 Be sociable.
Ethics	6.1.1 Be consistent in my educational values and my professional practice. 6.1.2 Welcome pedagogical initiatives.	6.2.3 Be fair. 6.2.4 Believe in the progress and professional development of each supervised person.
Emotional intelligence		6.2.5 Possess a strong sense of personal efficacy. 6.2.6 Manage my stress and emotions. 6.2.7 Consider the emotional and affective dimension of the supervised person and show empathy. 6.2.8 Be a good listener. 6.2.9 Make people comfortable and trusting.

Chapter Seven

The *Know How to Become* Every Supervisor Should Possess

Teaching supervisors help other educators to identify and develop their skills; however, these leaders also need opportunities and support to be able to broaden their own *knowledge, know how to do*, and *know how to be* (beliefs, values, attitudes, and hypotheses), which define and influence their supervision practices (Burns, Yendol-Hoppey, & Jacobs, 2015).

The supervisor is also entitled to have access to continuing education to help them be better guides for their teachers. In the spirit of continuous improvement, the supervisor must keep informed regarding reforms and new pedagogical practices, and closely follow how their school navigates through these waters and evolves. Developing their *knowing how to become* thus represents the first step toward strong pedagogical leadership (Peterson & Peterson, 2006).

Several professional development actions are thus recommended:

- participation in a PLC or professional practice community for supervisors;
- participation in a research-action-training project;
- participation in discussions with colleagues and education consultants on the relevance of didactic and pedagogical choices;
- reflective analysis of their own practice;
- documentation by consulting published research;
- participation in pedagogical networks and professional associations;
- development of their own professional portfolio;
- university continuing education, whether credited or not; and
- other training, whether online or in person.

The supervisor who enhances their knowledge base and relational skills acquired through their professional development and continuous training can therefore serve as a model for their teachers by preaching by example.

7.1—PEDAGOGICAL *KNOW HOW TO BECOME*

In this section, the following four pedagogical *know how to become* are examined:

- self-evaluate and identify my training needs in pedagogy and supervision;
- learn more about pedagogical innovations and winning trends in this field;
- develop my professional development program in pedagogy; and
- keep abreast of new theories and practices in teacher supervision.

7.1.1—Self-Evaluate and Identify My Training Needs in Pedagogy and Supervision

In some schools, the district superintendent or general director supports the professional development of the pedagogical supervisor. Their duty is to create joint conversations in which supervisors are able to reflect on and self-evaluate their capabilities (Zepeda, Lanoue, Creel, & Price, 2015).

Either alone or supported by their immediate superior, a good supervisor takes the necessary time to reflect on the practice to be able to provide more effective support to their supervised teacher. Indeed, the competent action of this educator lies in their ability to position themselves to perform better in situations, but it also emanates from their ability to reflect on this action (L'Hostie, Cody, Monney, Laurin, & Belzile, 2011).

The needs identified by means of a self-evaluation may be addressed through self-learning activities, such as reading and discussions with colleagues, among others, or by more formal training through active participation in professional development activities.

7.1.2—Learn More About Pedagogical Innovations and Winning Trends in This Field

As a result of the increasing interest in the pedagogical leadership of school principals, both practitioners and this research domain have been challenged to profoundly reflect on how educational activity can be better managed, on the impact of the supervisor's leadership on their teachers, and on how this leadership can be more effectively applied (Brassard et al., 2004).

Consultations within the current education system demonstrate the relevance of involving teachers. Many school-teams and supervisors welcome, recognize, and support the innovations of some of their teachers (Deslauriers, 2008). *Innovation* of course refers to an idea, a practice, or an object perceived as being new by the members of a system (Legendre, 2005). These teachers want to develop a spirit of collaboration with colleagues and peer evaluation practices, as well as work in collaboration with professionals within a shared or collegial culture (Lusignan, 2008). Surveys conducted with teachers reveal that they strongly believe in the importance of studying existing teacher supervision practices from the perspective of both the supervisor (principal, teacher-leader, or other) and the person being supervised, namely, the teacher (Tarakdjian, 2008).

The world of education is in constant evolution. It is only logical that the school leader also evolves by keeping informed on what works and what doesn't to remain competent, relevant, and credible in their actions. They must therefore also benefit from professional development to better guide their supervised teachers and have a good knowledge of winning pedagogical practices and advances in the fields of education and pedagogy (Marzano, Waters, & McNulty, 2016).

To be effective in their pedagogical role, the supervisor must continuously update and upgrade their supervision skills and keep abreast of teaching and learning reforms. One training priority is to be better equipped to implement these pedagogical reforms in their school. Arpin and Capra (2008) explained that the successful supervisor analyzes their practices, updates their knowledge base regarding learning theories, and uses research to support their actions, particularly data on teacher performance in the classroom.

7.1.3—Develop My Professional Development Program in Pedagogy

Our participating school leaders were emphatic: we are generalists, not specialists. The supervisor can, therefore, address pedagogical aspects without going into the didactics of a given subject, if the latter is not part of their personal field of expertise. For example, the supervisor must have knowledge of the general objectives of existing education programs and the main elements of teaching and practice methodologies outlined in these platforms without necessarily knowing all of the specific objectives and all of the teaching and learning assessment activities of each teacher.

7.1.4—Keep Abreast of New Theories and Practices in Teacher Supervision

In our research-action-training project, 65% of our participants received no formal training in teacher supervision. Considering that pedagogical supervision is among a principal's most important duties, it is imperative that supervisors seek out continuous professional development in the field of teacher supervision and take initiatives in this regard.

Whether formal or informal, what is important to remember is that continuing education must be experienced as perpetual research, reflection, and sharing.

7.2—*KNOW HOW TO BECOME* IN HUMAN RELATIONS

In this section, a single *know how to become* in human relations is examined: Learn more about human relations approaches.

7.2.1—Learn More About Human Relations Approaches

Pedagogical supervision is an approach defined by human relations between the supervisor and their supervised teacher. So how can this win-win relationship be successful?

Human relations approaches have a significant influence on both management and leadership style. This multifaceted model encompasses the supervisor's behavior with the supervised person, their approach to make the latter feel comfortable with the process, the quality of their interventions, the level of collaboration provided, and the trust developed. These approaches may include training initiatives, collaborative actions, motivational theories, communication, change management, diversity within the school (cultural, religious, generational, etc.), and emotional management.

For an overview of the *know how to become* of an effective supervisor, see Table 7.1.

Table 7.1. Synthesis of the Main *Know How to Become* of the Effective Supervisor

Know How to Become *Pedagogically*	Know How to Become *in Human Relations*
7.1.1 Self-evaluate and identify my training needs in pedagogy and supervision.	7.2.1 Learn more about human relations approaches.
7.1.2 Learn more about pedagogical innovations and winning trends in this field.	
7.1.3 Develop my professional development program in pedagogy.	
7.1.4 Keep abreast of new theories and practices in teacher supervision.	

Conclusion

This competency standards framework begins with a definition of the necessary skills of the pedagogical supervisor: *knowledge*, *know how to do*, *know how to be*, and *know how to become*. Several referenced school management studies support these key teacher supervision capabilities.

Because supervisors are called on to develop many different skills and forms of knowledge to ensure quality supervision for their teachers, other types of knowledge could have been added to the list of proposed competencies. That said, due to the interrelations between the different forms of knowledge presented, the categorization method employed in this manual does have its limits, as is evidenced in the complexity of the distinction between *know how to be* and *know how to do*.

To conclude, pedagogical supervisors must recognize that competence evolves throughout their professional life and that skills development furthers understanding, expertise, and accomplishment. With competence, however, comes a certain responsibility. It is thus the duty of the supervisor to reinvest every level of knowledge into becoming a better mentor and model of supervision for their teachers, both individually and collectively. We therefore strongly encourage every supervisor to develop their own annual or multiannual professional development plan that takes into account their career path, the school's priorities, and the future development of the education system.

References

Acheson, K., & Gall, M. (2003). *Clinical supervision and teacher development: Preservice and inservice applications* (5th edition). New York, NY: John Wiley & Sons.

Al-Bataineh, A., & Nur-Awaleh, M. (2000). *Keeping teaching fresh.* https://archive.org/stream/ERIC_ED453215/ERIC_ED453215_djvu.txt

Archambault, J., & Dumais, F. (2012). *Des données pour diriger et prendre des décisions.* Montréal, QC: Université de Montréal.

Archambault, J., & Garon, R. (2012). Prioriser l'apprentissage au primaire: oui, mais comment? *Le point en administration scolaire, 14*(2), 33–36.

Archambault, J., & Richer, C. (2007). Des moyens pour comprendre et s'approprier les changements à apporter à l'école. *Vivre le primaire, 20*(2), 24–26.

Arnold, L. R. (2016). "This is a field that's open, not closed": Multilingual and international writing faculty respond to composition theory. *Composition Studies, 44*(1), 72–88.

Arpin, L., & Capra, L. (2008). *Accompagner l'enseignant dans son parcours professionnel.* Montréal, QC: Chenelière Éducation.

Attinello, J. R., Lare, D., & Waters, F. (2006). The value of teacher portfolios for evaluation and professional growth. *NASSP Bulletin, 90*(2), 132–152.

Bandura, A. (2003). *L'autoefficacité: le sentiment d'efficacité personnelle.* Paris, France: De Boeck.

Barbès, P. (2001). *Je mène ma supervision: manuel pour la supervision de stage.* Montréal, QC: Saint-Martin.

Bass, B. M. (1985). *Leadership and performance beyond expectations.* New York, NY: The Free Press.

Bass, B. M., & Stogdill, R. M. (1990). *Bass and Stogdill's handbook of leadership: Theory, research, and managerial applications.* New York, NY: Simon & Schuster.

Beeken, L. A., Shmidt, B. J., & Beaver, D. A. (1992). *Ideas for teacher collaboration. What happens when teachers collaborate?* Berkeley, CA: National Center for Research in Vocational Education.

Bélair, L. M., Lebel, C., Sorin, N., Roy, A., & Lafortune, L. (2010) *Régulation et évaluation des compétences en enseignement vers la professionnalisation.* Québec, QC: Presses de l'Université du Québec.

Bernatchez, J. (2011). La formation des directions d'établissement scolaire au Québec: Apprendre à développer un savoir-agir complexe. *Télescope, 17*(3), 158–175.

Blanchard, K. H., & Hersey, P. (1996). Life-cycle theory of leadership. *Training & Development*, *50*(1), 42–47.

Bouchamma, Y. (2004a). Gestion de l'éducation et construction identitaire sur le plan professionnel des directeurs et des directrices d'établissement scolaire. *Éducation et francophonie*, *32*(2), 62–78.

Bouchamma, Y. (2004b). *Supervision de l'enseignement et réforme*. http://www.inrp.fr/biennale/7biennale/Contrib/longue/7300.pdf

Bouchamma, Y. (2006). School principals' perceptions of personal and professional efficacy with regards to teacher supervision in New Brunswick. *Journal of Educational Administration and Foundations*, *17*(2), 9–23.

Bouchamma, Y. (2007). Evaluating teaching personnel: Which model of supervision do Canadian teachers prefer? *Journal of Personnel Evaluation in Education*, *18*(4), 289–308.

Bouchamma, Y., April, D., & Basque, M. (2017). Les communautés d'apprentissage professionnelles : un mode de fonctionnement pour opérationnaliser la reddition de comptes. *Revista de Sociología de la Educación*, *10*(3), 397–414.

Bouchamma, Y., & Basque, M. (2012), Supervision practice of school principals: Reflection in action. *US-China Education Review B7*, 627–637.

Bouchamma, Y., Giguère, M., & April, D. (2016). *La supervision pédagogique: guide pratique à l'intention des directions et des directions adjointes des établissements scolaires*. Québec, QC: Presses de l'Université Laval.

Bouchamma, Y., Godin, M., Jenkins Godin, C., Lê, T.-H., & Kardouchi, M. (2005). Évaluation du personnel enseignant. Lévis, QC: Les éditions de la Francophonie.

Bouchamma, Y., Iancu H-D., & Stanescu, M. (2008). L'évaluation du personnel enseignant au Maroc, en Haïti et en Roumanie: Aimilitudes et différences. *Revue stiinta sportului*, *6*(67), 67–92.

Bouchamma, Y., & Michaud, C. (2014). Professional development of supervisors through professional learning communities. *International Journal of Leadership in Education: Theory and Practice*, *17*(1), 62–82.

Bouchamma, Y., Savoie, A., & Basque, M. (2012). The impact of teacher collaboration on school management in Canada. *US-China Education Review B5*, 485–498.

Bourbeau, V. (2010). *Attraction et rétention de la clientèle étudiante du cégep Lévis Lauzon* (Doctoral dissertation, École nationale d'administration publique).

Boutet, M., & Pharand, J. (2008). *L'accompagnement concerté des stagiaires en enseignement*. Québec, QC: Presses de l'Université du Québec.

Boutet, M., & Rousseau, N. (2002). *Les enjeux de la supervision pédagogique des stages*. Québec, QC: Presses de l'Université du Québec.

Boyer, M., Corriveau, L., & Pelletier, G. (2011). *Des compétences en action: référentiels et pratiques de formation pour des dirigeants de l'éducation*. http://www.fsedu.usj.edu.lb/docs/documentation/Boyer%20Ref-formation%202009.pdf

Bradberry, T., & Greaves, J. (2006). *The emotional intelligence quick book: Everything you need to know to put your EQ to work*. New York, NY: Simon & Schuster.

Bradberry, T., & Greaves, J. (2009). *Emotional intelligence 2.0*. San Diego, CA: TalentSmart.

Brassard, A. (2009). Le projet de loi 88: Ses implications sur l'autonomie de l'établissement et sur les relations entre les échelons du système. *Le point en administration de l'éducation*, *11*(3), 11–14.

Brassard, A., Cloutier, M., De Saedeleer, S., Corriveau, L., Fortin, R., Gélinas, A., & Savoie-Zajc, L. (2004). Rapport à l'activité éducative et identité professionnelle chez les directeurs d'établissement des ordres d'enseignement préscolaire et primaire. *Revue des sciences de l'éducation*, *30*(3), 487–508.

Brunet, L. (2005). Les conduites non éthiques au travail. In L. Langlois, R. Blouin, S. Montreuil, and J. Sexton (Ed.), *Éthique et dilemmes dans les organisations*. Sainte-Foy, QC: Presses de l'Université Laval.

Burke, P., & Krey, R. D. (2005). *Supervision: A guide to instructional leadership.* Springfield, IL: Charles C. Thomas Publisher.

Burns, J. M. (1978). *Leadership.* New York. NY: Harper & Row.

Burns, R. W., & Badiali, B. J. (2015). When supervision is conflated with evaluation: Teacher candidates' perceptions of their novice supervisor. *Action in Teacher Education, 37*(4), 418–437.

Burns, R. W., Yendol-Hoppey, D., & Jacobs, J. (2015). High-quality teaching requires collaboration: How partnership can create a true continuum of professional learning for educators. *The Educational Forum, 79*(1), 53–67. doi: 10.1080/00131725.2014.971990.

Chin, R., & Benne, K. (1991). Stratégies générales pour la production de changements dans les systèmes humains. In R. Tessier and Y. Tellier (Ed.), *Théories du changement social intentionnel. Participation, expertise et contraintes*. Québec, QC: Presses de l'Université du Québec.

Collerette, P., Pelletier, D., & Turcotte, G. (2013). *Recueil de pratiques des directions d'écoles secondaires favorisant la réussite des élèves*. Université du Québec en Outaouais. http://www.ctreq.qc.ca/wp-content/uploads/2013/10/Recueil-Pratiques-de-gestion-favorisant-la-r%C3%A9ussite.pdf

Cook, L., & Friend, M. (1993). *Educational leadership for teacher collaboration*. http://files.eric.ed.gov/fulltext/ED372540.pdf

Coombs-Richardson, R., & Rivers, E. S. (1998, March). *Collaborating for change: Building partnerships among teachers*. Paper presented at the Annual Meeting of the Association for Supervision and Curriculum Development. San Antonio, TX.

Cormier, S. (1995). *La communication et la gestion*. Sainte-Foy, QC: Presses de l'Université du Québec.

Cormier, S. (2002). *Guide d'autodéveloppement des compétences en communication*. Université du Québec à Montréal. http://www.oiq.qc.ca/Documents/DAP/guide-autodeveloppement-competences-communication.pdf

Courpasson, D., & Livian, Y. F. (1991). Le développement récent de la notion de compétence: glissement sémantique ou idéologie? *Revue de gestion des ressources humaines, 1*, 3–10.

Da Costa, J. L. (1993). *A study of teacher collaboration in terms of teaching-learning performance*. Paper presented at the Annual Meeting of the American Educational Research Association. Atlanta, GA.

Da Costa, J. L. (1995a). Teacher collaboration: A comparison of four strategies. *Alberta Journal of Educational Research, 41*(4), 407–420.

Da Costa, J. L. (1995b, April). *Teacher collaboration: The roles of trust and respect*. Paper presented at the Annual Meeting of the American Educational Research Association. San Francisco, CA.

Danielson, C. (2014). Framework for teaching. Retrieved from: http://www.campbell.k12.ky.us/userfiles/1654/Kentucky%20Adapted%20Danielson%202011%20Framework%20for%20Teaching.pdf

Dardenne, B. (2008). La cognition sociale. In A. Van Zantem (Ed.), *Dictionnaire des sciences de l'éducation* (pp. 66–70). Paris, France: Presses universitaires de France.

DeJaeghere, J. G., & Zhang, Y. (2008). Development of intercultural competence among US American teachers: Professional development factors that enhance competence. *Intercultural Education, 19*(3), 255–268.

De Nobile, J. J., & McCormick, J. (2008). Organizational communication and job satisfaction in Australian Catholic primary schools. *Educational Management Administration & Leadership, 36*(1), 101–122.

Derrington, M. L. (2016). Principals, policy, and practice: Supervision in the intersection. In S. Zepeda and J. Glanz (Eds.), *Re-examining supervision: Theory and practice* (pp. 129–145). Lanham, MD: Rowman & Littlefield.

Desjardins, R. (2002). *Le portfolio de développement professionnel continu.* Montréal, QC: Chenelière/McGraw-Hill.

Deslauriers, C. (2008). Une route pavée d'encre et de mots. *Vie pédagogique, 147,* 15–19.

Dionne, L., Lemyre, F., & Savoie-Zajc, L. (2010). Vers une définition englobante de la communauté d'apprentissage (CA) comme dispositif de développement professionnel. *Revue des sciences de l'éducation, 36*(1), 25–43.

Drago-Severson, E. (2012). New opportunities for principal leadership: Shaping school climates for enhanced teacher development. *Teachers College Record, 114*(3), n3.

Drago-Severson, E., Blum-Destefano, J., & Asghar, A. (2013). Learning and leading for growth: Preparing leaders to support adult development in our schools. *Journal of School Leadership, 23*(6), 932–968.

Drago-Severson, E., & Blum-DeStefano, J. (2016). *Tell me so I can hear you: A developmental approach to feedback for educators.* Cambridge, MA: Harvard Education Press.

Drucker, P. F. (1966). *The effective executive.* New York, NY: Harper & Row Publishers.

Ducommun, P. (2008). La supervision dans l'enseignement et dans la formation des enseignants. In M. Guyaz (Ed.), *Quelle évaluation des enseignants au service de l'école* (pp. 79–81). Neuchâtel, Switzerland: Institut de recherche et de documentation pédagogique.

Duffy, F. M. (2016). Organizational arrangements. Supervision and administration: Past, present, and future. In S. Zepeda and J. Glanz (Eds.), *Re-examining supervision: Theory and practice* (pp. 81–96). Lanham, MD: Rowman & Littlefield.

DuFour, R. (2004). What is a professional learning community? *Educational Leadership, 61*(8), 6–11.

Dupuich-Rabasse, F. (2006). *La gestion des compétences collectives.* Paris, France: L'Harmattan.

Dupuis, P. (2004). L'administration de l'éducation: quelles compétences. *Éducation et francophonie, 32*(2), 132–157.

Durand, T. (2000). L'alchimie de la compétence. *Revue française de gestion, 127,* 84–102.

Eaker, R. E., DuFour, R., & DuFour, R. (2004). *Premiers pas: Transformation culturelle de l'école en communauté d'apprentissage professionnelle.* Bloomington, IN: National Educational Service.

Éthier, G. (1989). *Managing excellence in education.* Québec, QC: Presses de l'Université du Québec.

Fink, E., & Resnick, L. B. (2001). Developing principals as instructional leaders. *Phi Delta Kappan, 82*(8), 598–610.

Fortin, T., & Pharand, J. (2005). La communication à l'avant-scène. In N. Rousseau (Ed.), *Se former pour mieux superviser.* Montréal, QC: Guérin Éditeur.

Frawley, J., & Fasoli, L. (2012). Working together: Intercultural leadership capabilities for both-ways education. *School Leadership & Management, 32*(4), 309–320.

Fullan, M. (2006). Leading professional learning. *The School Administrator, 63*(10), 10–14.

Fullan, M. (2014). *Le leadership moteur: Comprendre les rouages du changement en éducation.* Montreal, QC: Fondation Lucie et André Chagnon.

Gable, R. A., & Manning, M. L. (1997). The role of teacher collaboration in school reform. *Childhood Education, 73*(4), 219–223.

Gall, M. D., & Acheson, K. A. (2011). *Clinical supervision and teacher development.* Hoboken, NJ: John Wiley and Sons.

Gardiner, M. E., & Enomoto, E. K. (2006). Urban school principals and their role as multicultural leaders. *Urban Education, 41*(6), 560–584.

References

Garman, N., & Holland, P. (2016). Getting to the new work of teaching, learning, and supervision: Are we finally at the quantum moment? *Supervision: New Perspectives for Theory and Practice*, 43–62.

Gercek, S. E. (2007). "Cultural mediator" or "scrupulous translator"? Revisiting role, context and culture in consecutive conference interpreting. *Translation and its others. Selected papers of the CETRA research seminar in translation studies.*

Girard, L., McLean, E., & Morissette, D. (1992). *Supervision pédagogique et réussite scolaire*. Boucherville, QC: Gaétan Morin.

Glanz, J. (2006). *What every principal should know about ethical and spiritual leadership*. Thousand Oaks, CA: Corwin Press.

Glanz, J., and Zepeda, S. J. (Eds.). (2015). *Supervision: New perspectives for theory and practice*. New York, NY: Rowman & Littlefield.

Glickman, C. D., Gordon, S. P., & Ross-Gordon, J. M. (2013). *Supervision and instructional leadership: A developmental approach* (9th edition). Boston, MA: Allyn & Bacon.

Goleman, D. P. (1995). *Emotional intelligence: Why it can matter more than IQ for character, health and lifelong achievement*. New York, NY: Bantam Books.

Gordon, S. P. (2008). Dialogic reflective inquiry: Integrative function of instructional supervision. *Catalyst for Change*, *35*(2), 4–11. Retrieved from http://www.ed.psu.edu/catalyst.

Gordon, S. P. (2015). Framing instructional supervision. In J. Glanz and S. J. Zepeda (Eds.), *Supervision: New perspectives for theory and practice* (pp. 23–42). New York, NY: Rowman & Littlefield.

Gordon, S. P., & Boone, M. (2014). *Alternative approaches to educational leadership preparation: A call for integration*. Ypsilanti, MI: National Council of Professors of Educational Administration.

Guillemette, S. (2011). *Contexte social et légal du rôle et des responsabilités de la direction d'établissement* (Unpublished doctoral dissertation). Université de Sherbrooke, Quebec, Canada.

Guillemette, S., Morin, F., & Simon, L. (2015). Une démarche de questionnement pour une gestion différenciée de l'activité éducative. *Formation et profession*, *23*(3), 45–56.

Hajisoteriou, C. (2012). Listening to the winds of change: School leaders realizing intercultural education in Greek-Cypriot schools? *International Journal of Leadership in Education*, *15*(3), 311–329.

Halawah, I. (2005). The relationship between effective communication of high school principal and school climate. *Education*, *126*(2), 334.

Hallier, J. (2009). Rhetoric but whose reality? The influence of employability message on employee mobility tactics and work group identification. *The International Journal of Human Resource Management*, *20*(4), 846–848.

Hallinger, P. (2005). Instructional leadership and the school principal: A passing fancy that refuses to fade away. *Leadership and Policy in Schools*, *4*(3), 221–239.

Hallinger, P., & Heck, R. H. (1998). Exploring the principal's contribution to school effectiveness: 1980–1995. *School Effectiveness and School Improvement*, *9*(2), 157–191.

Hargreaves, A., & Fink, D. (2006). *Sustainable leadership*. San Francisco, CA: Jossey-Bass.

Hazi, H. M., & Rucinski, D. A. (2009). Teacher evaluation as a policy target for improved student learning: A fifty-state review of statute and regulatory action since NCLB. *Education Policy Analysis Archives*, *17*, 5.

Heck, R. H., Larsen, T. J., & Marcoulides, G. A. (1990). Instructional leadership and school achievement: Validation of a causal model. *Educational Administration Quarterly*, *26*(2), 94–125.

Heck, R. H., Marcoulides, G. A., & Lang, P. (1991). Principal instructional leadership and school achievement: The application of discriminant techniques. *School Effectiveness and School Improvement, 2*(2), 115–135.

Heckman-Stone, C. (2003). Trainee preferences for feedback and evaluation in clinical supervision. *The Clinical Supervisor, 22*, 21–33.

Hersey, P., Blanchard, K. H., & Natemeyer, W. E. (1979). Situational leadership, perception, and the impact of power. *Group & Organization Management, 4*(4), 418–428.

Hétu, J.-L. (2007). *La relation d'aide. Éléments de base et guide de perfectionnement* (4th edition). Montréal, QC: Gaétan Morin.

Holland, N. E. (2002). *Small schools making big changes: The importance of professional communities in school reform*. Annual Meeting of the National Association of African American Studies, the National Association of Hispanic and Latino Studies, the National Association of Native American Studies, and the International Association of Asian Studies. Houston, TX.

Houle, H., & Pratte, M. (2003). Les conseillères et les conseillers pédagogiques. Qui sont-ils? Que font-ils? *Pédagogie collégiale, 17*(2), 20–26.

Howden, J., & Kopiec, M. (2002). *Cultivating collaboration: A tool for instructional leaders*. Montréal, QC: Chenelière/McGraw-Hill.

Huffman, J. B., & Hipp, K. K. (2003). Professional learning community organizer. In J. B. Huffman and K. K. Hipp (Ed.), *Professional learning communities: Initiation to implementation*. Lanham, MD: Scarecrow Press.

Inger, M. (1993a). Teacher collaboration in secondary schools. *Center Focus, 2*(1–4).

Inger, M. (1993b). *Teacher collaboration in urban secondary schools*. ERIC/CUE Digest, 93. New York, NY: ERIC Clearinghouse on Urban Education.

Janosz, M., Georges, P., & Parent, S. (1998). L'environnement socioéducatif à l'école secondaire: Un modèle théorique pour guider l'évaluation du milieu. *Revue canadienne de psychoéducation, 27*(2), 285–306.

Jay, M. (2003). Critical race theory, multicultural education, and the hidden curriculum of hegemony. *Multicultural Perspectives, 5*(4), 3–9.

Kanouté, F., Vatz Laaroussi, M., Rachédi, L., & Tchimou Doffouchi, M. (2008). Familles et réussite scolaire d'élèves immigrants du secondaire. *Revue des sciences de l'éducation, 34*(2), 265–289.

Kaser, J., Mundry, S., Stiules, K., & Loucks-Horsley, S. (2011). *Leadership scolaire au quotidien: 124 actions pour enrichir sa pratique*. Montréal, QC: Chenelière Éducation.

Kiemele, J. (2009). *Culturally proficient leadership: Intercultural sensitivity among elementary school principals*. Tempe, AZ: Arizona State University.

Kinkead, J. C. (2006). *Transformational leadership: A practice needed for first-year success*. Online submission. (ERIC Document Reproduction Service No. ED492009).

Klar, Hans W., Huggins, Kristin S., & Roessler, Amy P. (2016). Fostering distributed instructional leadership: A strategy for supporting teacher learning. In S. Zepeda and J. Glanz (Eds.), *Re-examining supervision: Theory and practice* (pp. 7–21). Lanham, MD: Rowman & Littlefield.

Knapp, M. S., & Feldman, S. B. (2012). Managing the intersection of internal and external accountability: Challenge for urban school leadership in the United States. *Journal of Educational Administration, 50*(5), 666–694.

L'Hostie, M., Cody, N., Monney, N., Laurin, N., & Belzile, S. (2011). L'agir compétent de l'enseignant associé en situation de stage. In F. Guillemette, J. Labelle, V. Freiman, and Y. Doucet (Eds.), *La communauté d'apprentissage professionnelle: Une démarche fa-*

vorisant la réussite éducative des élèves doués? (pp. 62–83). Québec, QC: Presses de l'Université du Québec.

Langlois, L., & Lapointe, C. (Eds.). (2002). *Le leadership en éducation: Plusieurs regards, une même passion.* Québec, QC: Chenelière McGraw-Hill.

Lapointe, P., & Archambault, J. (2013). L'engagement des directions dans la gestion pédagogique de l'école. *Le point sur le monde de l'éducation, 16*(1), 50–51.

Lapointe, P., Brassard, A., Garon, R., Girard, A., & Ramdé, P. (2011). La gestion des activités éducatives de la direction et le fonctionnement de l'école primaire. *Revue canadienne de l'éducation, 34*(1), 179–214.

Lauzon, N., & Madgin, L. (2003). L'évaluation des ressources humaines. In J.-J. Moisset, J. Plante, and P. Toussaint (Ed.), *La gestion des ressources humaines pour la réussite scolaire* (pp. 235–266). Québec, QC: Presses de l'Université du Québec.

Le Boterf, G. (2002). *Développer la compétence des professionnels* (4th edition). Paris, France: Éditions de l'Organisation.

Le Boterf, G. (2011). *Ingénierie et évaluation des compétences* (6th edition). Paris, France: Eyrolles.

Lebrun, M., Smidts, D., & Bricoult, G. (2011). *Comment construire un dispositif de formation?* Brussels, Belgium: De Boeck.

Leclerc, M. (2010). Diriger une école en la centrant sur la communauté d'apprentissage. *inDirect. Les clés de la gestion scolaire* (Brussels, Belgium), *19*(1), 32–56.

Leclerc, M., Moreau, A., & Lépine, M. (2009). *La communauté d'apprentissage professionnelle pour améliorer l'apprentissage des élèves en lecture: Mieux comprendre les stades de développement.* 16th Conference européenne sur la lecture (ERA), Braga, Portugal.

Legendre, R. (2005). *Dictionnaire actuel de l'éducation* (3rd edition). Montréal, QC: Guérin.

Leithwood, K., & Jantzi, D. (2000). The effects of transformational leadership on organizational conditions and student engagement with school. *Journal of Educational Administration, 38*(2), 112–129.

Leithwood, K., Leithwood, D., & Daniel, L. (1998). Mapping the conceptual terrain of leadership: A critical point of departure for cross-cultural studies. *Peabody Journal of Education, 73*(2), 31–50.

Leithwood, K. A., & Riehl, C. (2003). *What we know about successful school leadership.* Nottingham, UK: National College for School Leadership.

Leurebourg, R. (2013). Rôles des directions d'école de langue française en situation minoritaire. *Revue canadienne de l'éducation, 36*(3), 272–297.

Levenson, N. (2011). Declining resources, targeted strategies. *School Administrator, 68*(1), 10–17.

Levin, B., & Fullan, M. (2008). Learning about system renewal. *Educational Management Administration & Leadership, 36*(2), 289–303. doi: 10.1177/1741143207087778.

Liontos, L. B. (1992). Transformational leadership. *ERIC Digest, 72.* http://files.eric.ed.gov/fulltext/ED347636.pdf

Lortie, C., & Héon, F. (2005). La nouvelle génération de leaders. *Le Soleil*, section Économie, votre emploi.

Loufrani-Fedida, S., & Saint-Germes, È. (2013). Compétences individuelles et employabilité: Essai de clarification de leur articulation. *GRH, 2*(7), 13–40.

Louis, K. S., Leithwood, K., Wahlstrom, K. L., Anderson, S. E., Michlin, M., & Mascall, B. (2010). Learning from leadership: Investigating the links to improved student learning. *Center for Applied Research and Educational Improvement/University of Minnesota and Ontario Institute for Studies in Education/University of Toronto, 42*, 50.

Lucas, S. E., & Valentine, J. W. (2002). *Transformational leadership: Principals, leadership teams, and school culture.* http://files.eric.ed.gov/fulltext/ED468519.pdf

Lusignan, G. (2008, May). Rencontre avec Pierre Lebuis, formateur en éthique et culture religieuse. *Vie pédagogique, 147*, 3–7.

MacNeil, A. J., Prater, D. L., & Busch, S. (2009). The effects of school culture and climate on student achievement. *International Journal of Leadership in Education, 12*(1), 73–84.

Mailhot, C. (2010). La convention collective: Une bible ou un outil de travail? *Le point en administration de l'éducation, 12*(2), 10–12.

Marks, H. M., & Printy, S. M. (2003). Principal leadership and school performance: An integration of transformational and instructional leadership. *Educational Administration Quarterly, 39*(3), 370–397.

Marzano, R., Waters, T., & McNulty, B. (2016). *Leadership scolaire: De la recherche aux résultats.* Québec, QC: Presses de l'Université du Québec.

Maslow, A. H. (1943). A theory of human motivation. *Psychological Review, 50*(4), 370.

Maxwell, J. C. (2003). *Leadership. 101 principes de base. Ce que tout leader devrait savoir.* Nashville, TN: Un monde différent.

McEwan, E. K. (1997). *Leading your team to excellence: How to make quality decisions.* Thousand Oaks, CA: Corwin.

McGlynn, C. (2009). Negotiating cultural difference in divided societies. In *Peace Education in Conflict and Post-Conflict Societies* (pp. 9–25). New York, NY: Palgrave Macmillan.

McKee, A., Boyatzis, R., & Johnston, F. (2011). *Propulser mon équipe grâce à l'intelligence émotionnelle.* Montréal, QC: Éditions Transcontinental.

McShane, S. L., & Benabou, C. (2008). *Comportement organisationnel: Comportements humains et organisations dans un environnement complexe.* Montréal, QC: Chenelière McGraw-Hill.

Melchers, D. (2005). *De gestionnaire à leader.* Sherbrooke, QC: GGC Éditions.

MIC, recrutement de cadres. *La culture organisationnelle et le leadership.* http://www.micexecutifs.com/Documentation/Culture.html

Moisset. J.-J., Plante. J., & Toussaint, P. (2003) *La gestion des ressources humaines pour la réussite.* Montréal, QC: Transcontinental.

Newmann, F. M. (1994). School-wide professional community. *Issues in Restructuring Schools, 6*, 1–2.

Nolan, J. F., & Hoover, L. A. (2004). *Teacher supervision and evaluation: Theory into practice* (2nd edition). Hoboken, NJ: Wiley.

Northouse, P. G. (2007). *Leadership: Theory and practice* (4th edition). Thousand Oaks, CA: Sage Publications.

Ogolla, P. A. (2003, January). *Practicing elementary teachers' perspectives of "investigations" curriculum.* Paper presented at the Annual Meeting of the American Association of Colleges for Teacher Education. New Orleans, LA.

Pack-Brown, S. P., Thomas, T. L., & Seymour, J. M. (2008). Infusing professional ethics into counselor education programs: A multicultural/social justice perspective. *Journal of Counseling & Development, 86*(3), 296–302.

Paquay, L. (2007, December). *Vers quelles évaluations du personnel enseignant pour dynamiser leur développement professionnel et leur implication vers des résultats?* Leysin, Switzerland: AIDEP.

Pastor, P., & Bréard, R. (2004). *Diriger une équipe: les clés du succès.* Paris, France: Éditions Liaisons.

Pelletier, G. (2006). *Le leadership suivant la contingence des situations.* Forres. http://docplayer.fr/4710787-Le-leadership-suivant-la-contingence-des-situations.html

Peterson, K. D., & Peterson, C. A. (2006). *Effective teacher evaluation: A guide for principals.* Thousand Oaks, CA: Corwin.

Poirel, E. (2009). *Le stress professionnel, les émotions vécues et les ajustements chez les directions d'école au Québec.* Fédération Québécoise des directions d'école. http://fqde.qc.ca/wp-content/uploads/2014/02/Stress-Emmanuel-Poirel.pdf

Ponticell, J. A. (2015). A retrospective look at data embedded in instructional supervision. *Supervision: New Perspectives for Theory and Practice*, 163.

Prairat, E. (2013). *La morale du professeur.* Paris, France: Presses universitaires de France.

Pugach, M. C., & Johnson, L. J. (1995). *Collaborative practitioners, collaborative schools.* Denver, CO: Love Publishing Company.

Quinn, J. B. (1992). The intelligent enterprise: A new paradigm. *Academy of Management Executive*, *6*(4), 48–63.

Reed, C. (2003). Principal self-efficacy and effective teaching and learning environments. *School Leadership & Management*, *23*(4), 505–508.

Reyes, P., & Fuller, E. J. (1995). *The effects of selected elements of communal schools on middle and high school mathematic achievement* (Research Report No. 142). Madison, WI: Center on Organization and Restructuring of Schools and Wisconsin Center for Education Research.

Rhodes, C., & Beneicke, S. (2002). Coaching, mentoring and peer-networking: Challenges for the management of teacher professional development in schools. *Journal of In-Service Education*, *28*(2), 297–310.

Ribas, W. B. (2005). *Teacher evaluation that works!!: The educational, legal, public relations (political) & social-emotional (ELPS) standards & processes of effective supervision & evaluation.* Westwood, MA: Ribas Publications.

Riordan, G. P., & Da Costa, J. L. (1996, April). *Self-initiated high school teacher collaboration.* Paper presented at the Annual Meeting of the American Educational Research Association. New York, NY.

Roberts, S. M., & Pruitt, E. Z. (2003). *Schools as professional learning communities.* Thousand Oaks, CA: Corwin Press.

Ross, M. (2012). *Les compétences de directions d'école efficace: Études de cas dans deux écoles secondaires québécoises* (Unpublished doctoral dissertation). Université Laval, Quebec City, Canada.

Rousseau, N. (2005). *Se former pour mieux superviser.* Montréal, QC: Guérin éditeur.

Roy, P., & Hord, S. M. (2006). It's everywhere, but what is it? Professional learning communities. *Journal of School Leadership*, *16*, 490–501.

Safourcade, S., & Alava, S. (2009). S'autoévaluer pour agir: Rôle du sentiment d'efficacité personnelle dans les pratiques d'enseignement. *Questions vives*, *12*, 109–123.

Saint-Germain, M. (2002). Le leadership constructiviste: Une solution au paradoxe de l'individualité et de la normalisation. In C. Lapointe and L. Langlois (Eds.), *Leadership en éducation, plusieurs regards, une même passion* (pp. 113–138). Montréal, QC: Chenelière/McGraw-Hill.

Sangsue, J., & Vorpe, G. (2004). Influences professionnelles et personnelles du climat scolaire chez les enseignants et les élèves. *Psychologie du travail et des organisations*, *10*(4), 341–354.

Savoie-Zajc, L. (2008). L'accompagnement dans la démarche de projets développés par le milieu scolaire pour soutenir la persévérance et la réussite scolaires : étude des besoins et de la dynamique. [En ligne] : http://www.frqsc.gouv.qc.ca/documents/11326/449042/PT_SavoieL_rapport+2010_%C 3%A9tude+besoins+de+dynamique-soutien+PRS/a7004ba0-0e26-4a0e-b20e0b4b9d005c35

Schermerhorn, J. R., Hunt, J. G., Osborn, R. N., & de Billy, C. (2014). *Comportement humain et organisation* (5th edition). Saint-Laurent, QC: Renouveau Pédagogique Inc.

Scott, S. (2004). *Fierce conversations: Achieving success at work & in life, one conversation at a time* (2nd edition). New York, NY: Berkley Publishing.

Sergiovanni, T. J. (2001). *Leadership: What's in it for schools?* New York, NY: Routledge Falmer.

Sergiovanni, T. J., & Starratt, R. J. (2006). *Supervision: A redefinition* (8th edition). New York, NY: McGraw-Hill Higher Education.

Serres, G. (2009). Analyse de l'activité de supervision au regard de ses effets sur la trajectoire de formation des professeurs stagiaires. *Éducation et francophonie, 37*(1), 107–120.

Shank, M. J. (2006). Teacher storytelling: A means for creating and learning within a collaborative space. *Teaching and Teacher Education, 22*(6), 711–721.

Slater, L. (2005). Leadership for collaboration: An affective process. *International Journal of Leadership in Education, 8*(4), 321–333.

Smith, S. C., & Scott, J. J. (1990). *The collaborative school: A work environment for effective instruction*. Eugene, OR: Clearinghouse on Educational Management, University of Oregon; Reston, VA: National Association of Secondary School Principals.

Spraker, J. (2003). *Teacher teaming in relation to student performance: Findings from the literature*. Portland, OR: Northwest Regional Educational Lab.

Stevens, F. I. (1997). *Opportunity to learn science: Connecting research knowledge to classroom practices*. Philadelphia, PA: Mid-Atlantic Lab for Student Success and the National Research Center on Education in the Inner Cities.

Sullivan, S., & Glanz, J. (2000). *Supervision that improves teaching: Strategies and techniques*. Thousand Oaks, CA: Corwin Press.

Tannenbaum, R., & Schmidt, W. H. (1973). *How to choose a leadership pattern*. Boston, MA: Harvard Business Review.

Tarakdjian, É. (2008). Évaluation des compétences professionnelles en collégialité. *Vie pédagogique, 147*, 52–55.

Tardif, N. (2005). Indicateurs du climat organisationnel dans les établissements d'enseignement. Notes du cours ADS 802 Développement organisationnel, Université de Sherbrooke.

Tate, C. A. (2010). Revenue in public higher education: A dean's perspective. *Quest, 62*(1), 10–14.

Tillman, L. C. (2002). Culturally sensitive research approaches: An African-American perspective. *Educational Researcher, 31*(9), 3–12.

Toffler, A. (1990). *Powershift: Knowledge, wealth and violence at the edge of the 21st century*. New York, NY: Bantam Books.

Tremblay, M. B. (1999). *L'empathie comme modèle de communication dans l'enseignement aux adultes : une recherche heuristique*. (Mémoire de maîtrise inédit). Université du Québec à Chicoutimi.

Tremblay, M., & Simard, G. (2005). La mobilisation du personnel: L'art d'établir un climat d'échanges favorable basé sur la réciprocité. *Gestion, 30*(2), 60–68.

Tschannen-Moran, M., Uline, C., Woolfolk Hoy, A., & Mackley, T. (2000). Creating smarter schools through collaboration. *Journal of Educational Administration, 38*(3), 247–272.

Tucker, P. D., Stronge, J. H., Gareis, C. R., & Beers, C. S. (2003). The efficacy of portfolios for teacher evaluation and professional development: Do they make a difference? *Educational Administration Quarterly, 39*(5), 572–602.

Vachon, I., Guertin, D., & Jutras, F. (2013). La compétence conjuguée: Une avenue pour la collaboration interprofessionnelle entre directions d'établissements scolaires et conseillers pédagogiques. *Le point sur le monde de l'éducation, 6*(1), 42–43.

Wang, M. C., Haertel, G. D., & Walberg, H. J. (1993). Toward a knowledge base for school learning. *Review of Educational Research*, *63*(3), 249–294.

Wang, M. T., & Degol, J. L. (2016). School climate: A review of the construct, measurement, and impact on student outcomes. *Educational Psychology Review*, *28*(2), 315–352.

Watson, S. C. (2001). Institutional responses to adult students: Candid comments from students. *The Journal of Continuing Higher Education, 49*(2), 23–32.

Weisinger, H. (2013). *L'intelligence émotionnelle au travail*. Montréal, QC: Les éditions Transcontinental.

Wilhelm, A. (2013). Obstacle externe et obstacle interne à la supervision. *Revue de psychothérapie psychanalytique de groupe*, (2), 79–87.

Witherspoon Arnold, N. (2016). Cultural competencies and supervision: New perspectives for theory and practice. In S. Zepeda and J. Glanz (Eds.), *Re-examining supervision: Theory and practice* (pp. 201–220). Lanham, MD: Rowman & Littlefield.

Ylimaki, R. M. (Ed.). (2014). *The new instructional leadership: ISLLC Standard Two*. New York, NY: Routledge.

Zepeda, S. J. (2006). High stakes supervision: We must do more. *International Journal of Leadership in Education*, *9*(1), 61–73.

Zepeda, S. J. (2012). *Instructional supervision: Applying tools and concepts* (3rd edition). New York, NY: Routledge.

Zepeda, S. J. (2013). *The principal as instructional leader: A practical handbook* (3rd edition). New York, NY: Routledge.

Zepeda, S. J. (2016). *The leader's guide to working with underperforming teachers: Overcoming marginal teaching and getting results*. New York, NY: Routledge.

Zepeda, S. J., Lanoue, P. D., Creel, W. G., & Price, N. F. (2015). Supervising and evaluating principals. In S. J. Zepeda and J. Glanz (Eds.), *Re-examining supervision: Theory and practice* (pp. 241–268). Lanham, MD: Rowman & Littlefield.

About the Authors

 **Yamina Bouchamma**, PhD, is full professor in the Department of Foundations and Practices in Education at Université Laval. Her academic activities, research interests, and publications notably regard the competencies of school administrators and pedagogical supervision.

 **Marc Giguère**, MEd, is lecturer in the Department of Foundations and Practices in Education at Université Laval. He has extensive experience as principal in both primary and secondary education. His expertise also includes the professional development of school leaders.

 **Daniel April**, PhD, serves as research and communications consultant at the United Nations Educational, Scientific and Cultural Organization (UNESCO) for the Global Education Monitoring Report (GEM). He holds masters and doctorate degrees in educational administration and policy studies from Université Laval as well as a BEd in French second-language education.